It Can Never Get Too Cold

(And Other Minnesota Humor)

by

Mary E. Hirsch

Published in the United States by Mary E. Hirsch

www.swellthoughts.com

Second Edition

Dedicated to Jean who took all the clipped articles and retyped them for me during her unemployment period -- at no charge -- she won't even let me buy her breakfast.

And to my mom who clipped and saved everything I had published and kept them in a nice folder in her desk.
I love you mom and miss you every single day.

And to my dad who left this world way too soon and I never got to share my writings with him. His friends and family say I have his sense of humor and fun and
I love him and miss him every single day.

And, of course, also to my boyfriend Keifer Sutherland, even though he doesn't know he's my boyfriend.

It Can Never Get Too Cold

Chapter 1
Doing The Lakes

My first publication ever was with the *Southwest Journal* and I will always be grateful to Janis Hall and Mark Anderson for having faith in a newbie and letting me have a column called "Doing the Lakes." I was lucky enough to find them when they were just starting the newspaper and got in on the ground floor. I'm sure part of their willingness was the fact that they needed copy and I worked cheap.

"Doing the Lakes" is based on the fact that people in the area "do the lake" the same way people "do lunch," "do coffee," or "do dah, do dah." While many people live near a lake, more people have to travel to get there – and travel they will. On a nice day they migrate in herds from the suburbs to "do the lake." If you aren't careful you can easily be run over by a minivan, a sports car, or a piece of crap that is being held together by duct tape and a prayer (most likely a Lutheran prayer).

I grew up three blocks from Lake Harriet and have always lived pretty close by. I did move closer to the mansion-circled Lake of the Isles where I fit in like a red plaid shirt at a black tie party and recently moved back into a 'hood that is more "me."

Writing instructors and books always say "write what you know" so I wrote about Minnesota instead of physics, painting, or anything even slightly domestic.

A Rite of Spring -- Doing The Lake

Now that the ice on the lakes has melted and the sight of your breath no longer resembles the by-product of the downtown garbage incinerator, people are again drifting toward the area lakes to become part of one of the rites of spring: doing the lake.

Doing the lake is not about getting back to creation or becoming one with the Universe. No! Doing the lake is more. Doing the lake is a sociological, economical and political act. It is networking with nature. If one wants to succeed in this world (this world being the immediate seven-county metro area to be precise), one must not only do the lake, one must do the lake correctly.

This column, Lake Breaking News, will deal with the pertinent issues of lake doing. It will help the lake ignorant blend in with the lake elite; it will give lake alumni some new ideas as well as open a new world to the lake virgin. For if one is going to go to all the trouble of laking, one might as well derive all the benefits laking affords them.

While future columns will deal with the tangibles of laking (dress, accessories, fine dining, pathway etiquette, social interaction, etc.) and tangibles are important, this edition of Lake Breaking News will deal with the intangibles of laking; of embracing the lake and making it part of your being. You must become the lake!!!

Many support groups have surfaced to help people achieve lakeness. The most prominent such group is BOWL (Bonding Ourselves With Lakes). BOWL seeks to lead people from the shores of self-doubt into the waves of self-ecstasy; to comb the beaches of their souls and detect the real mettle of their being.

But BOWLers must first admit they are powerless over the lake; that their lives and often their hair have become unmanageable. They must sink to the bottom before they can float on top.

Many tools are available to people who want to internalize the lake:

1. The CD "You Are The Lake" features subliminal messages such as:
- You are the lake; you are all wet.
- You are the lake; you are shallow.
- You are the lake; you are washed up

This CD is available at local bookstores and will be featured at the lake refectories.

2. The best-selling book by lake therapist Dr. Millie Dew entitled "Dipping Your Toes In the Whirlpool of Life; or How to Spread Your Waterwings and Fly." Dr. Dew will be signing copies of her book every Thursday this summer on the third bench after the Port-O-Pot.

3. Aroma Therapy disks are available to help you breathe lakeness into your being. A few examples are A.M. Algae, Seaweed Winds or Dead Fish Desire.

4. Well-known lecturer Richard "My Friends Call Me Dick" Johnson will give a four part series in the public library meeting room: "Skimming the Lake, Skimming My Psyche: Breaking the Bubbles of Defeat."

It Can Never Get Too Cold

These are only a few of the many opportunities available to those who want to take their laking seriously. Prepare now to become a laker (Minneapolis laker not L.A. Laker). This season when you show up on the shores be one of those people whom others point to and stare at, whom cars slow down to gawk at, whom children follow. Be a person who says "I Am A Laker."

Warning: The Surgeon General has determined that the lake should not be taken internally on the physical dimension of a being. It has the toxic level of Sylvester Stallone's bath water. The lake should only be internalized on a spiritual dimension, even if you were a rhinoceros in a past life.

Mary E. Hirsch

A Holiday Shopping Guide For The Lake Lover
On Your Gift List

With the holiday season here it is time to think about what to buy the lake-crazy person in your life. You know, that special someone who is constantly at the shores of one of our city lakes. Doing the Lakes Products is happy to present some unique gifts for the laker in your life.

• This year, give that fishing fanatic of yours a subscription to Good Icehousekeeping. Each issue is packed with features such as:

- tuck-away auger cabinets you can make yourself
- kerosene heater potpourri
- quick-to-crochet fishing pole covers
- gourmet hot plate meals

and much, much more. A gift subscription to Good Icehousekeeping will make any laker smile.

• On those clear, brisk evenings when you can't resist a walk by the lake, you'll be glad you have on the Steer Clear Ear Muffs. Not only will these muffs keep your ears warm, but when the built-in radar detector senses a low flying plane approaching, a hidden antenna will emerge with flashing red arrows to indicate to the passing aircraft that this is not the runway…do not land here…proceed to the airport. And, as an added bonus, the muffs have been insulated for sound with the same materials MAC uses to insulate homes in the airport pathway. The Steer Clear Ear Muffs have been approved by the FAA.

• The canine walker in your life will sit up and say "Thanks" when you give the Pucci Bag. Everyone knows even the greatest lake outfit looks tacky when accessorized with

9

an old plastic bread bag tied to a leash. Now, thanks to Doing the Lakes Products, there's The Pucci Bag. Just strap this designer dog-dropping bag onto your doggie's leash and tuck that unsightly plastic bag inside until its ready to be used. Pull it out, pick it up and pop it back inside. The charcoal lining goes to work absorbing those unpleasant odors until the doggie's "do" can be properly disposed of, and all the time – you look good! Put The Pucci Bag on your shopping list this year.

- Every year there is one book that continually appears on the best seller list for Doing the Lakes Products, and "What Color is Your Fanny Pack" will be no exception.

This book is the complete guide for the person who suddenly finds laking has lost its thrill and is thrown into a mid-lake crisis:

"Should I continue jogging or really get into spandex and take up windsurfing?" "The kids are gone and I'm left with water-wings, a sand pail and shovel, and a lot of extra time. What should I do?" "Every year it's the same old thing, ride the trolley, eat some popcorn. Being at the lake has lost its meaning."

If there's someone on your gift list who could use a little help, "What Color is Your Fanny Pack" gives the guidance needed for any person traveling the lake paths of life.

- For the man in your life who goes the distance, Doing the Lakes Products introduces Maráthoné cologne. Created in the gymnasiums of Greece, Maráthoné keeps going strong when other colognes have hit the wall. One whiff of the Maráthoné man and that special someone's heartbeat will be racing at aerobic levels. So if there's a hunka-hunka running love in your life, you'll want to put Maráthoné on your shopping list.

• Move over Sports Illustrated, here comes Doing the Lakes Products "Hunks and Hunkettes of the Lake" calendar. Imagine how exciting your year will be when you share it with Fishin' Fred, Joggin' Judy, Trolley Travis and nine other luscious lakers. Each calendar comes with special event stickers that list significant lake events such as the unlocking of the bathroom facilities, the day the Dangerous Thin Ice signs go up, and the opening of metal detecting season. Give a year of fun with this great gift.

• It won't be winter forever – really! So Doing the Lakes Products suggests a bottle or two of Lake 'n Bake Suntan Lotion. Lake 'n Bake not only contains moisturizers for beautiful soft skin but it is the only suntan product that contains mosquito repellent because it won't be winter forever.

• And don't forget that when you are invited to that important holiday party, you can impress everyone with your good taste when you say "I'll have a glass of Pump." Yes, Pump Sparkling Water is fresh from the lake pumps. A refreshing glass of Pump with a twist of lemon will help make your holiday bright. And for a limited time only, Doing the Lakes Products brings you Pump in a holiday designer jug. Pick up a jug or two to have on hand when unexpected company stops by.

Let Doing the Lakes Products help make your holiday a laker's dream come true.

All The World Is A Dock And We Are Only Trollers

Many of you will soon find in your mailbox the announcement of the upcoming Tyrone Guthrie Theater season. But before you send in your season ticket order, consider your local community theater: Doing the Lakes Theater and Bait Shop.

This season follows on the heels of its greatest year ever playing to sellout crowds and the accolades of critics. If you missed last year's production you missed "Mulch Ado About Nothing," "Breath of a Salesman," "My Picnic With Andre," "Night of the Iguanathon," "Duck on a Hot Tin Roof," and, of course, "The Icehouse Cometh." This year promises to be even more exciting. Founder and create director Myron Algae has chosen six plays specifically with the lake community in mind:

The season starts with "**Parkinlot.**" This whimsical tale comes to life on the stage where we are transported back to the kingdom of Parkinlot – a mythical time and place filled with sky blue pavilions and refreshment stands. Watch as King Fraser's Knights of the Picnictable valiantly battle with Volvonian dragons that have descended from Mt. Suburbia for parking spaces at the lake on beautiful Saturday afternoons.

No matter how many times you've seen "**My Airfare Lady,**" you'll still have fun watching as disposable diaper entrepreneur Henry Huggies attempts to transform Liza Dogdolittle from a runway-wise baggage handler to an airport commissioner. You will feel your heart pounding at that pivotal point when, after hours of drilling, Liza loudly declares: "The harangue of planes drives many to complain." (By George we think she's got it!!) And your eyes will brim again as the young air traffic controller who has fallen so deeply in love with Liza declares his adoration in the classic song:

> I have often walked down this street before.
> But the pavement never shivered to the airplane roar
> All at once am I, staring at the sky,
> Knowing I'm on the flight path where you live.

Next we turn our stage over to "**The Grass Menagerie**." This classic by playwright Minnesota Williams will touch your heart. It is an intimate look at the imaginary world of Laura, a lonely woman whose only friends are her collection of Chia-like pets covered with growth from the transplanted clippings of her yard. Laura stands on the hedge of moving forward but her hopes are mowed down and her prospects for happiness trimmed when she mistakes a sales representative from On Our Turf Lawn Service for the gentleman gardener her brother said would be visiting.

Speaking of classics, is any theatrical season complete without the revival of a Renaissance classic? We know our production of Lakespeare's "**Rolleo and Joggiet**," the love story of love stories, will touch you as if you were seeing it for the first time. Return to see the balcony scene where Rolleo, the only child of the Wheeler family, stands waiting for the appearance of his love Joggiet, the only child of the Nike family. As Rolleo and Joggiet transcend the feud between their families and swear their cross-my-heart-training love for each other, you will wonder at the inevitable tragedy caused by the senseless feud between these families over who has the right of way on a lake path.

And what better way to show the eternal truth of the Rolleo and Joggiet story than with the modern day adaptation "**Southwest Side Story**." Here, instead of rival families we find love developing between Tole and Melena, members of The Crappies and The Bass – rival fishing gangs. You will be stunned by the beauty and power of the choreography in the rumble scene at the fishing dock. Perhaps you'll even find yourself singing along:

> When you're a Bass you're a Bass all the way
> From your first casting off to your last-caught filet
> When you're a Bass let 'em wade if they can,
> You got buddies around; You're a fly fishin' man.

"Southwest Side Story" undoubtedly will be a favorite this year so be sure your seat is reserved.

To close the season you'll be glad you have reserved seat when you see "**Pumping Iron Magnolias**." The story of seven women who meet every day at muscle beach to develop and strengthen their bodies and relationships. You will be drawn into their world as they go for the burn, go for the gusto, and go for it all because their stories are really the stories of all us lakers who are going for it all. (Except most of us get worn out pumping water and can't wear a thong swimsuit.)

Be sure to order your tickets today for the Doing the Lakes Theater and Bait Shop season and discover that all lake culture isn't visible only under a microscope.

Mary E. Hirsch

Summer Reading Includes New Editions of Old Favorites for the Doing The Lakes Crowd

Forget the Doubleday Book Club; say goodbye to The Literary Guild; bid a fond farewell to the Book of the Month Club – it's time to become a member of the Doing The Lakes Book Club.

Once a month (whether you want it or not) you will be sent a new selection for your reading pleasure. Each book is chosen with the lake lover in mind. Enjoy each selection for 10 days and if after 10 days you decide you don't like the book – too bad. You'll just have to keep it, pay for it and put it on your bookshelf with all the other books you haven't read.

Here is a look at upcoming selections:

East of Eatin': The tale of two handsome and fiercely competitive brothers enmeshed in an ice cream war. Follow their lives as they travel the roads in their refrigerated wagons filled with deep dark chocolate and deep dark secrets. These venomous vendors are not just looking for hungry stomachs; they're looking for hungry hearts.

The Algae Also Rises: An intriguing story of a free-spirited fishing trip guide who comes of age when his courage is tested at the running of the bullheads in Pamplona Bay.

The Accidental Bicyclist: Here is the story of Norm, an author of books focusing on bicycle paths around the world, and how his world changes when he meets Breeze, a free-spirited manicurist who helps him risk riding through life without training wheels.

Mommy Deerest: The dramatic story of Jessica Fawn, who was separated from her parents in a Hennepin County Reserve Park, where she was found and raised by Joan Doe, a famous but domineering and self-centered deer. Jessica really bucks the system in this revealing book.

The Lake Path Less Traveled: This self-help book is for anyone who wants to shift from traveling the familiar lake paths of life where they find themselves moving but always ending up in the same place to paths that lead them to new inlands and peninsulas of the soul.

Rabbit is Deaf: When famous lounge act Sonny Rabbit moves his family to a house on the airport flight path, he finds the roar of engines has left him more than tone deaf; he can't hear the applause he lives for.

Little Icehouse on the Prairie: Your heart will be touched by the story of the Anglers – Pa, Ma, and their three little minnows – as they struggle against all odds to become a family in their wooden shack that is warmed with love and a portable heater.

Catch-23: For the fishing addict in your house, here is the ultimate fishing guide. A few hours with this beautifully illustrated book and soon you'll be catching your limit every day.

The Power of Positive Sinking: Has life left you feeling like you're in over your head and you've grown tired of treading water? Then this inspirational book is what you need to see how to inflate your ego so you too can float toward the seas of success.

The Witches of East Parkway: There's something brewing on East Parkway when three longtime friends Harriet, Calli and Cedar meet Bill Z. Bub, the new trolley car conductor, who gives a fresh meaning to the term "speed demon."

Windsurfers of War: An epic novel about the Navy's commando surfing squad headed by Capt. Moondoggie. You will be mesmerized by his attempts to defend democracy at the same time he's trying to catch a WAVE named Ensign Gidget.

The Godfeather: The story of the notorious Mallard family and its leader – the Donald. This flock is into everything from smuggling Columbian duckweed to selling Quack and any rival who sets a webbed foot into their territory will soon find his goose is cooked.

Don't delay. Act now. If you join today your first selection will include, free of charge (except for an exorbitant shipping and handling fee), the best seller **Fear of Fly Fishing**, an erotic novel that has been banned in Milaca, Duluth and Brainerd.

Doing The Lakes Has A Fall Class
For You

Doing The Lakes Community Center (sponsored by Doing the Lakes Products) is pleased to announce its Fall community education schedule. We hope you Lakers will take advantage of one of our many offerings:

Icehouse Repair and Maintenance: This four-week class will cover topics ranging from how to smooth out the edges on your fishing hole, caulking ice cracks, proper plywood care, and building hooks to hang your hats on. As a bonus we will have a guest lecture on "How To Keep Your Beer Cold And Your Feet Warm."

Floatus 1-2-3: For the true fishing fanatic this computer program was specially designed by Doing the Lake Products to give you all the tools you need for a fishing venture that is always successful. You will learn to take all the important factors of fishing into consideration: water, depth, current and temperature, spawning patterns, bait choice, and the hours and locations of the nearest fish market.

Crochet a Bench Cozy: Winter is just around the corner and just because ice and snow are on the benches doesn't mean Jack Frost has to be nipping at your derriere if you want to sit and enjoy a few minutes at the lakes. You will learn to crochet an attractive and functional bench cozy that has been designed especially for this class by Doing the Lakes Products. Each cozy contains storage pouches for a magazine, a thermos of coffee, and duck food keeper.

Sandcastle Building: Have you ever felt inadequate when you compare your sand castle to the one built by the four-year-old next door? Isn't it humiliating enough to have a properly pumped up bully kick over your sand castle without having him laugh at it too? If so, this class could be just what you need to show up all the kiddies and bullies at the lakes. Each student will design and build a castle from one of the many blueprints available from Doing the Lakes Products. This three-week class will give you the skill you need to return to the sand next spring without an umbrella of shame hanging over you.

Lake Sign Language: Ever speculated what those gestures people give you as you drive around the lakes at 10 mph really mean? Have you ever wondered if that sly smile on the jogger who just passed you by was a come-on or gas? By the end of this course you will know what people are really saying even if they don't know what they are saying.

With Mallard-Malice Towards None: Are you harboring a grudge or two against some of our web-footed residents? Is stepping in duck droppings starting to get under your feathers? Have you recently been chased by a crazed goose? Then this one-week session may help you to understand our fine-feathered friends. A guided meditation will lead us to the ponds of our minds where you will experience what it is like to be a duck, and to see the world from a duck's perspective. By the end of this session you and the ducks of the world will be as one.

Seaweed Sculptures: This class brings together the ecological and arts communities in order to find a productive use for the algaes polluting our lakes – other than weird back-to-nature casseroles and breads. Using various mediums from paraffin to brass you will create sculptures imbedded with deep symbolism and dripping with irony. The unknown seaweed sculptor of today could be the creator of tomorrow's Venus de Milfoil.

The Waddling Gourmet: Tired of throwing out a few stale bread crumbs and popcorn kernels to our lakes' fowl residents? This two-week class will help you to create international treats that will have those duck bills watering. What duck worth its feathers could resist a handful of Russian Gorp-a-chow or a sprinkling of Columbian Cracked Wheat Nibblers? Watch as the flocks paddle past those old cereals in favor of your Pasta Quackavera. Other lakers will feel embarrassed to be seen hurling Wonder bread balls when you are serving up Nacho Cheese and Ducko Chips. Before long word of your culinary prowess will have traveled by word of bill and ducks will be coming from all over the city to have one of your famous meals.

How to Get Your Adorable Child Noticed At the Lake: There is nothing worse than showing up at the lake with your adorable offspring all dressed up, and have no one take notice of his or her preciousness. What's the point of even going to the lake if you aren't going to get any attention for your child? This seminar will teach you foolproof methods to gain attention such as how to nonchalantly push a buggy into a stranger's stomach causing him or her to bend over and take a good look at your kid; child face manipulation for the cutest possible expressions; darling phrases to teach your child to say to passing joggers ("Look Momma, it's Superman" being a perennial attention getter); and the ten most popular stuffed animals to gain the attention of passers-by. After this seminar the only people at the lake who won't take notice of your child are parents jealous of all the attention your progeny is generating, or who have also taken this class. Register quickly, this class fills up fast!

Refectory Reflections: Here is a safe harbor for the budding memoirist to unleash the water muse from within. You will inline skate to your soul and find yourself caught in a trolley named desire as you liberate your feelings onto the blank page. This class will pump the spring waters of your mind and let you flow with words of ecstasy. Be sure to bring a number 2 pencil, a three-ring ¾" notebook, and a packet of 3x5 notecards to the first class – which will begin promptly at 7:00.

Remember Lakers, education is a never-ending process. Don't let the trolley car of your mind jump the track. Sign up today.

Get Ready for the Doing The Lakes
Winter Olympic Games

This winter the eyes of the world will be on the Winter Olympics. But for those of you who would like to experience the chill of victory and the agony of de-frozen feet a little closer to home, for the unofficial Doing The Lakes Winter Olympics. Here local residents are unknowingly competing for the Cold, Shiver and Breeze medals in events you'll never see on ESPN.

Snowbank Hurdles: The snowplows have come (finally) and gone (again) and you are left with a 10-foot embankment to climb in order to get to your car. This is an event that requires coordination, determination and the instinct of a mountain goat (not to mention hip boots and a compass).

Intersection Slide: Competing minivans come together at a four-way stop covered with a sheet of ice. Who will stop? Who will slide? Who will get a major increase in their car insurance rates?

Neighbor Recognition: A well-padded human form ap-proaches you. It is waving and appears to know who you are. All you see are two watery eyes peering at you from inside this cocoon with legs. Its words of greeting are muffled from underneath a scarf and warm air mask. Quick – name this neighbor!

Push or Tow: A team competition requiring individuals whose most well developed muscles to date are in the fingers they use to push the remote control buttons for their televi-sion set. In a team effort, these individuals will attempt to free automobiles stuck in five feet of snow before the city tow trucks show up.

Window Scraping: A thick layer of ice has formed on the windows of your car. It will take three hours for your defroster to work its way through the mini-glacier and you are already late for work. This is an event that requires aerobic elbows, saintly patience, surgical skills and the ability to drive while peering through a hole the size of a piece of lefse. The person who gets to their destination first (without an accident of a serious nature) wins.

Bus Running: MTC commuters line up at the starting line – half a city block from the bus stop. The bus is at the corner picking up those overachievers who left the house on time. Briefcase in one hand, an All You Can Ride Card frantically waving in the other hand, who can get to the corner before the bus pulls away without: a) swearing; b) falling; c) slipping; or d) being hit by the car of a neighbor participating in the previously discussed Window Scraping event who is now driving on sheer faith.

Mitten Match: Parents are faced with a six-foot-high pile of mittens, gloves, scarves, hats, socks and underpants. At the sound of the school bus backfiring three blocks away, each competitor has two minutes to dress three children in winter wear that actually belongs to them and goes together before the school bus passes their corner.

Pothole Dodge: This cross country event has auto athletes traveling local snow emergency routes covered with potholes that have been cleverly camouflaged as smooth pavement. Driving over, around and into these potholes earns points for each Olympian based on the degree of difficulty and incline of the pothole. At the end of winter these points are tallied and a winner is determined by a combination of points scored and the estimate from a certified mechanic for a front-end alignment.

Weatherizing: Using a standard window sealing kit from 3M® (an unofficial sponsor of winter), each participant in the weatherizing competition must cover a six-by-three-foot picture window and securely seal it with a blow dryer before the spring thaw sets in. Points are awarded for speed of application, flair of dryer handling, non-use of foul language, and air current testing. In addition the judges will award points for clarity based on the ability to recognize objects outside the window after the film has been applied. (If you can't tell the difference between Aunt Thelma standing on the curb and a stalled pickup parked in front of the house, you will receive no points.)

And finally, what would the Unofficial Doing The Lakes Winter Olympics be without the main event. **Augering:** Here ice fishing fanatics test their drilling skills as they bore their way to glory. Points are awarded not just for speed of completion, precision of hole size, and artistry of style. Points are also earned for the compulsory 250-word essay titled "Why I Love To Stand Out In The Freezing Cold Staring Into a Hole In The Ice Waiting For a Fish to Bite On My Line When I Could Be At Home Watching Television and Drinking Beer."

So the next time you find yourself engaging in one of these unofficial Olympic events, hold your head up high and be proud of being a Doing The Lakes Olympian. (But don't hold your head too high in case an Alberta clipper blows off your hat or you slip on an icy spot on the pavement.)

Don't Be A Victim! Use These Tips For Staying Safe At The Lakes

1. When getting out of your car, don't yell to your waiting friend: "I'll be there in a minute. I just have to put my purse filled with lots of money under my fur coat in the trunk so no one will take it."

2. No matter how much you like the noise, don't put an American Express Gold Card in the spokes of your bicycle.

3. If you are attacked don't yell "Help" or even "Fire"; no one may come. Instead yet – "Walleye, Walleye," and you will be surrounded in a matter of minutes.

4. If you hear heavy breathing coming up behind you don't assume it is a runner – it could be an asthmatic mugger or a pervert who is a heavy smoker.

5. When using one of the portable toilet facilities, always lock the door and check under the lid – you never know who could be hiding in there

6. In order to avoid being hit, if you are at the lake after dark, wear reflective clothes. Better yet, carry a sign saying: Airport Due West – Do Not Land Here.

7. Don't take candy from strangers. However, if you are offered pepperoni pizza or Haagen-Dazs chocolate chocolate chip ice cream you will have to use your best judgment.

8. Don't leave valuables in your car, especially if you have a bumper sticker that reads: I Brake For Stockbrokers.

9. Don't wear a fanny pack with compartments labeled: Sparking Water, Mercedes Keys, Diamonds, and Credit Cards.

10. If a stranger pulls up along you on the road and asks for directions don't approach the car. Instead yell, "Do I look like a GPS?" and keep moving.

11. When at a band concert don't announce loudly – "I love this song. You should hear it on my new compact disc quadraphonic player that I have in my unlocked Porsche parked around the corner with the keys left in it."

12. Don't be fooled by con artists trying to sell you a city permit to wear spandex in public. This permit can only be purchased at City Hall.

13. Beware of people with fishing poles begging for money to buy food; they will probably just spend it on bait.

14. Don't wear a tee shirt that says – "I'm An Out of Shape Wimp Carrying a Lot of Cash."

15. Even if he has a vendor's license, don't buy a hot dog from anyone named Roadkill Ralph (or let him take care of your dog while you are out of town).

16. Don't jog in high heels. Not only could you seriously hurt yourself, but if you don't have a matching handbag and pearls you could look incredibly tacky.

17. Assume everyone is a potential attacker and stay away from them. This is especially helpful if you happen to run into your mother-in-law, boss, or an evangelist.

18. If a duck approaches you and asks what time it is don't be fooled – he may only be checking to see if you are wearing a Rolex.

19. Be careful of people soliciting funds for phony charities. For example, the mosquito is not an endangered species and there is no treatment center for people who fish too much (although there should be).

20. Don't get suckered into a phony gambling scheme. Beach Blanket Bingo is a movie, not a new Minnesota scratch-and-win game.

Hopefully these guidelines will enable you to have a safe time at our city's lakes.

Some Stores For The Minneapolis Lakes Crowd

Between online shopping and the Mall of America it is likely that a local store will have to combine neighborhood charm with megamall glitz to bring in the customers. Some possible shops that might work in the neighborhood:

White Flight Travel. In one convenient location, individuals can find the what they will need to travel permanently from the city to the suburbs – real estate agents, moving companies, styling gel, and white bread.

Waders. Move over Hooters, this is a seafood restaurant where the waiters really know how to fill out a rubber fishing ensemble.

Mace-Eze. An assortment of safety-in-a-canister for the discriminating consumer who wants protection – and more. For example, the person seeking something that makes a fashion statement as well as defends may want to purchase an interchangeable carrying case for a mace canister. And, for the environmentally-minded, there's a pump canister rather than an aerosol spray so you can defend yourself without hurting the ozone layer.

Mr. Field N. Stream's Cookies. Manly, yet gourmet, cookies that go great on any hunting or fishing trip. Filled with nuts and baked on a Weber Grill, these snacks say "Macho" with every bite.

Skeeter Bytes. There's always something buzzing around at this computer store – a breeding ground for electronic products in the city of lakes.

Sneers. The department store where grumpy and suspicious America shops.

Camp Snobby. An amusement park where the elite meet featuring: Limo Loop – a stretch roller coaster that travels up through Haughty Hills and down to Condescending Acres; Lake Superiority – a water ride where passengers travel in a 12-foot Perrier bottle; Bumper Autos, where drivers in BMWs and Mercedes crash into one another and then try to file a lawsuit before the other driver; and the Let Them Eat Cake Bakery where exceptional pastries can be purchased and consumed.

What's Up Dock? In conjunction with state HMOs and the DNR this is the world's first combination medical/fishing clinic. The fishing fanatic patient can be treated at the clinic for high blood pressure while learning to filet a walleye.

Fowl Plays. A local dinner theater featuring the works of Arthur Mallard and other Pouletry Prize playwrights.

Streetcar's Desire. Here you can find intimate apparel for your car such as a snug-fitting satin teddy for the driver's seat or a steering wheel cover made of black leather and decorated with simulated diamonds.

High Loons. An outpatient treatment center for hunters who can't stop at their limit.

Lutefisk Bell. An exclusive café featuring lutefisk burritos, lutefisk nuggets, lutefisk fajitas, and the ever popular You Betcha Meal for kids.

It Can Never Get Too Cold

Chapter 2

Winter

People who don't know a lot about Minnesota know one thing for sure – it is cold during the winter. People who live here also know it is cold during the winter but apparently we don't care enough to leave. The comedian Lewis Black has said that the severe cold temperatures in Minnesota are not weather they are an emergency situation and we should demand that the government relocate us temporarilty to some place warm – like 20° .

My theory is anyone who stays in Minnesota use to be a bear in another life – we know all about winter hibernation and accept it as part of life. Many people find things to do in the snow so they can "enjoy" the season – I know they are lying but I won't attack their delusion because they may come after me with a sharp auger. The rest of us stay inside as much as possible and complain (and/or write) about the cold – we are the ones who are in touch with our true feelings. We are also the ones who cause an unbelievable spike in the sales of cookies and liquor in the Minnesota area. Hey, until you've dunked your Oreo in bourbon you don't know what you're missing.

How Cold Is It?

Tired of wind chill factors, below-freezing temperatures, and Fahrenheit-hype? This year, when you're asked how cold it is, say it's colder than:

• A limo ride with Amy Klobuchar and Michele Bachmann

- Frosty the Proctologist's fingers

- The phones at a Save the Rich telethon

- A set of snare drums at a Gregorian chant festival

- A bowling alley that just ran out of beer

- A tow truck driver's heart on a snow-emergency night

- A romantic evening at Home Depot

- A DMV clerk's stare

- The dance floor at an Amish wedding

- An outhouse seat in International Falls

- A hospital's reception to an uninsured patient

- The behind of a klutzy skater

- A romance novel written by Jessie Ventura

Pack Your Bags

During a Minnesota winter there are several *I-need-a-vacation* signs you'll want to keep in mind. You can be certain it's time to head south when:

1. Your skin is the same color as Papa Smurf's.

2. You feel naked without the flaps of your hat over your ears.

3. You are drafting a prenuptial agreement with the snowman in the front yard.

4. You've decided to grow a beard for warmth – but your husband complains it tickles.

5. You are crocheting mufflers for all of the snowplow drivers in the city.

6. You swear you can see Elvis's face in your bowling ball.

7. Polka music has become an aphrodisiac.

8. You've just noticed what a pretty mouth your goldfish has.

9. You are considering becoming an addict just so you can go someplace and get a group hug.

10. You attach yourself to a hot chocolate IV.

11. You are writing a one-person show based on the life of your guinea pig Taffy.

12. You are anxiously awaiting the *Sports Illustrated* snowsuit edition.

Prepare Now and Avoid the Onset of Cabin Fever

It is November. The trick or treaters have come and gone, Park Board soccer and football have ended, a good share of the population past age 67 has left for the Sunbelt, and the last signs of autumn (streets covered with fallen leaves, flattened squirrels and decimated pumpkins) are slowly disappearing. Yes winter is coming – and by January almost every Minnesotan will be suffering a social disease no antibiotic can cure: Cabin Fever.

Cabin fever sets in right after the holidays, when the initial thrill of shoveling, starting your frozen car, locating mittens, and blow-drying your windows has worn off. It is a time when virtually every New Year's resolution you made has been broken and Land's End has the nerve to send you its spring and summer catalog. It is that time of year when no one goes out unless they have to, and then it is usually to stockpile junk food, get new movies, go ice fishing, get beer, or pick up a refill on your antidepressant.

Maybe this year could be different. Maybe this will be the year when cabin fever won't get the best of you and your family. Here are some activities that may help you make it through another winter.

• Learn to make shadow puppets of Minnesotans who have been elected President of the United States.

• Suggest that your kids read a classic and then spend the rest of the winter bugging them to do it.

• Write a Haiku rap song in Norwegian.

- Make duck decoys out of the fruitcake Aunt Mildred sent you.

- Start a campaign to bring back the 8-track tape.

- Learn all the words to "Hail Minnesota," then try to get on "America's Got Talent to sing it.

- Hide one piece of a 500-piece jigsaw puzzle and then suggest that your family put the puzzle together as a group project.

- Develop a YouTube show featuring your dog refusing to go outside.

- Bake dozens of rich, fatty, chocolate cookies for shut-ins – and then eat them all yourself.

- Learn sign language – this will be helpful as you travel the highways next summer.

- Go down to the lake, find a duck you can relate to, and establish a special bond.

- Open your front door when it is below freezing, go call your mom and tell her "Guess what – I'm heating the great outdoors!"

- Carve the head of your favorite Power Ranger out of oatmeal.

- Learn how to properly floss your teeth.

• Watch "The Sound of Music" over and over again until Julie Andrews starts to look like Michele Bachmann and you find yourself rooting for the Gestapo.

If all of this fails to get you out of the winter doldrums, you may want to invite some friends over – like Ben and Jerry, Sara Lee, Betty Crocker, Chef Boyardee, the Three Musketeers...

The Snowman Cometh - And Protesteth

If there are children living in a house in Minnesota, more than likely there will be a snowman on the front lawn sometime during the winter. But the life of snowmen isn't easy. Here are their main complaints:

1. Snow women are frigid.

2. Rabbits are constantly nibbling at our noses.

3. Second-hand smoke from corncob pipes.

4. Dogs treating us like second-class hydrants.

5. Just 'cause we're roly-poly doesn't mean we're always jolly, happy souls.

6. We're tired of wearing funny-looking red plaid hats.

7. Is Frosty the only name you idiots can think of?

8. Snow angels yelling, "Hey, Twig Arms, wanna play catch?"

9. Getting pelted with snow blower debris.

10. The constant scraping sound of shovels against the sidewalks.

11. Never being able to get really rad clothes in our sizes.

12. Getting icicles stuck in our teeth – with no dental floss in sight.

13. We can't spring break in Fort Lauderdale.

14. Being spray painted by rival snowman gangs.

15. We're tired of people not understanding the depth and meaning of Robert Frost.

Think Winter is Long and Boring?
Think of All the Wonderful
Pleasures the Season Brings

Now that fall is over bringing the inevitable start of winter – and all the grumbling that accompanies it, it may be a good time to think of all the wonderful things winter brings us:

1. Swimsuit season is so far away we can always begin our diet tomorrow.

2. There are fewer bike thefts (and it is easier to catch someone trying to ride away on your bike when they are pedaling through 10 foot drifts with their long underwear caught in the bike chain).

3. It is perfectly acceptable to lay on the couch watching television with an old blanket over you – it is your contribution to conserving our natural resources.

4. Every day holds the promise that tomorrow you won't have to go to work or school because it could be a snow day.

5. It is easier to get an outside table at your favorite restaurant.

6. There is always some kind of excuse why you can't go and visit your in-laws (the car battery is dead, the garage door is frozen shut, there was no place to park on the even or odd side of the street, etc.)

7. You can watch all those PBS specials you recorded over the summer.

8. The danger of getting malaria from a mosquito bite is much lower.

9. The elections are over.

10. You can read all the magazines that piled up in the corner until you found time to get to them. (Spoiler alet: World War II is over!)

11. You can finally get those flabby upper arms into shape by scraping ice off your car windows.

12. When your kids say they are bored you can always suggest that they go outside and shovel.

13. The beaches aren't as crowded.

14. You always know what the temperature is in International Falls, Minnesota.

15. You won't be awakened early on Saturday morning by your neighbor's lawnmower.

16. People won't think you're lazy because you still have Christmas lights up on your house.

17. You don't have to wait so long for a tennis court at the park.

18. It's easier to pick up dog deposits from your yard.

19. Those flaky relatives from Florida, California, etc. will not come to stay with you for weeks.

20. You can wear plaid flannel shirts without being asked if you are related to Paul Bunyan.

21. Very few people will tell you how they hate the humidity.

22. It's easy to find a parking spot at the lake.

23. You can't hear the airplanes as well over the hum of snow blowers and snow plows.

24. Tan lines refer to the various shades of brown suits at Macy's.

25. The risk of death from killer bee attacks is minimal.

26. It's a good time to start that hair replacement project before hat season ends.

27. Hot fudge sundaes are medical necessities to prevent hypothermia.

28. Your mid-life crisis will be put on hold until convertible season begins again.

Mary E. Hirsch

To Be A Well-Adjusted Minnesotan, You Must Accept These Wintry Facts of Life

Have you ever met people who have spent their entire lives in a place where it is always warm and when they discover you are from Minnesota they say "I don't know how you can stand to live where it is so cold!" (And they usually say it in such a way that makes it sound like not only are you cold but you are also nine pins short of a strike.)

What these people don't understand is that living in a cold climate is a matter of accepting certain facts of life. Anyone who has lived in Minnesota for a few winters knows the basic Winter Chill Factoids. These are:

1. When waiting for a bus, the wind will always blow from the direction you have to face in order to watch for your bus.

2. Your car battery will go dead the day after your auto club membership expires.

3. The snow plow will come down your street right after you have finished clearing out your driveway.

4. The wind chill is always adjusted in relation to your age. For example, if you are 60 the wind chill is always at least sixty degrees colder than they tell you on the radio.

5. You will run out of windshield washer fluid as a convoy of 50 semi-trailers drive past you.

6. It will not snow again if you buy a new snow blower.

7. Your office will declare a snow day when you are on vacation.

8. It will snow in Florida while you are vacationing there.

9. There will be an ice storm while your relatives are visiting.

10. You will find your lost glove on the first day of spring.

11. There are no attractive winter hats.

12. Every parent will tell their child at least once, "Close the door – we aren't heating the great outdoors."

13. Everything will be closed down during a snow storm except your bank, which will process checks that you can't cover because you can't get to the bank to make a deposit.

14. Meteorologists will say "Brrrrrrr, it's a chilly one!" at least 50 times.

15. You will develop such a bad case of cabin fever you will spend an entire weekend watching all the movies of Don Johnson.

16. One of your kids will use your car brush as a hockey stick and fail to return it to your car. You will not discover this until you have to remove six inches of heavy, wet snow with your hands.

17. You will remember too late that it is not smart to hold your car keys in your mouth in sub-freezing weather.

18. An attorney from Dial L-A-W-Y-E-R-S will slip on the ice on your steps.

19. On the day when you are sure you will finally make a big breakthrough in therapy, the roads will be impassable and your appointment will be canceled.

20. You will have at least one embarrassing moment due to static cling.

'Twelve Weeks of Winter' Shows the Reasons We Love the Season

I'm not a winter person. I suppose I should move to Arizona but I have a feeling if I did all hell would break loose in the ozone layer and Minnesota would be dry and warm and Arizona the freezer chest of the earth. Besides, I like it here. After all, where else can a person say "You betcha I'd love some hotdish" without getting a few stares?

I don't hate winter, I just don't get very excited when it shows up. It's kind of like when you were a kid and your aunt came for dinner – you knew it wouldn't kill you but you were glad when it was all over.

Some things I like about winter include:

1. Snow at Christmas (which is the winter equivalent of saying, "I love the heat but hate the humidity");

2. Not feeling guilty about staying home and watching television instead of doing something more productive like jogging, finding a cure for cancer, or studying a romance language;

3. Not having to explain that cellulite is really a sign of incredible sensuality; and

4. The occasional snow day when you don't have to go to work because you aren't "essential" (which has the added benefit of letting you know your place on the corporate ladder).

Some things I dislike about winter include:

1. Not being able to complain about the humidity or highway construction (this leaves me with very little small talk for elevator rides, so I then get the urge to use the stairs, which could lead to exercise and I can't stand that thought at all);

2. Having my hair and dress stand on end as they become victims of the static wars (which tends to leave me looking like a Don King exhibitionist);

3. Getting all bundled up only to discover I have to go to the bathroom (don't pretend it has never happened to you); and

4. Feeling like I should have a "winter" hobby like needlepoint, jigsaw puzzles, or chopping wood.

So since I am resigned to another winter in Minnesota (which is my own decision so don't expect to see me on Dr. Phil's upcoming segment of Women Who Are Trapped in Minnesota), I have written yet another rip-off of "The Twelve Days of Christmas," which I call "The Twelve Weeks of Winter":

On the first week of winter the season brought to me, an orange stripe around my Dutch elm tree.

On the second week of winter the season brought to me two fender dents and an orange stripe around my Dutch elm tree.

On the third week of winter the season brought to me three snow drifts, two fender dents and an orange stripe around my Dutch elm tree.

It Can Never Get Too Cold

On the fourth week of winter the season brought to me four icy tumbles, three snow drifts, two fender dents and an orange stripe around my Dutch elm tree.

On the fifth week of winter the season brought to me Five Cold Things (use your imagination), four icy tumbles, three snow drifts, two fender dents and an orange stripe around my Dutch elm tree.

On the sixth week of winter the season brought to me six gloves a missing, Five Cold Things, four icy tumbles, three snow drifts, two fender dents and an orange stripe around my Dutch elm tree.

On the seventh week of winter the season brought to me seven gutters brimming, six gloves a missing, Five Cold Things, four icy tumbles, three snow drifts, two fender dents and an orange stripe around my Dutch elm tree.

On the eighth week of winter the season brought to me eight weeks of cable, seven gutters brimming, six gloves a missing, Five Cold Things, four icy tumbles, three snow drifts, two fender dents and an orange stripe around my Dutch elm tree.

On the ninth week of winter the season brought to me nine strains of virus, eight weeks of cable, seven gutters brimming, six gloves a missing, Five Cold Things, four icy tumbles, three snow drifts, two fender dents and an orange stripe around my Dutch elm tree.

On the tenth week of winter the season brought to me ten more pounds to cope with, nine strains of virus, eight weeks of cable, seven gutters brimming, six gloves a missing,

Five Cold Things, four icy tumbles, three snow drifts, two fender dents and an orange stripe around my Dutch elm tree.

On the eleventh week of winter the season brought to me eleven parking tickets, ten more pounds to cope with, nine strains of virus, eight weeks of cable, seven gutters brimming, six gloves a missing, Five Cold Things, four icy tumbles, three snow drifts, two fender dents and an orange stripe around my Dutch elm tree.

On the twelfth week of winter the season brought to me twelve 50 minute sessions of intensive psychotherapy to help me relieve my winter anxiety level, eleven parking tickets, ten more pounds to cope with, nine strains of virus, eight weeks of cable, seven gutters brimming, six gloves a missing, Five Cold Things, four icy tumbles, three snow drifts, two fender dents and an orange stripe around my Dutch elm tree.

The worst is yet to come. At the end of winter brings the worst phenomenon known to humankind – the beginning of bathing suit shopping season.

Winter and its Silver Linings (!!*@!!!*#%!!!)

There is a certain group of gleeful individuals who delight in snowfalls and record low temperatures.

They obviously include the people who sell snow blowers, thermal underwear, cold and flu medications and car-starting devices.

I also have a sneaking suspicion that the meteorologists on the local television stations are enjoying themselves. There is a sort of scary Stephen King kind of look in their eyes when they say the "coldest Christmas ever," or "bundle up, we have temperatures that will be dipping waaaaaaaaaay below zero tonight."

And those guys who give you the traffic report on the radio just whip themselves into a freezing frenzy when the driving conditions are bad. It's like they wait all year for a semi to jack-knife and block an off ramp, "causing major delays for commuters heading in that direction."

But for the rest of us, who hang in there, winter after winter, knowing that there is a thaw somewhere on the horizon, this is a difficult time of year.

Of course, one nice thing about this kind of weather is you always have something to say to a stranger. In the summer we say "Boy it's sure hot. I don't mind the heat, it's the humidity I can't stand." In the winter we say, "I don't mind the snow, it's the cold I can't stand." Keeps us from having to bear that awkward silence during an elevator ride.

Bad weather gives Minnesotans a sense of continuity,

something we can always complain about. But instead of complaining about the weather, isn't it time we try to look for the silver lining in those winter clouds?

For example, I have cold-induced asthma. Sure it can be a nuisance not being able to breathe, but on the bright side, I have found that during a severe attack, I am able to wheeze the entire score of "Oklahoma." It's not just a disease, it's performance art. It never fails to delight the numerous emergency-room attendants I've had the pleasure to meet.

Since I've been able to find the silver lining in my winter cloud, I thought I could help all of you find something good about winter, too.

• The next time you take off your hat and find your hair has taken on a life of its own, don't think of it as hat hair, think of it as an emergency generator that can be used in case of a power outage. Why, you may be able to produce enough electricity to keep your DVD player working for a showing of great Minnesota winter movies, such as "Fargo," "Grumpy Old Men," "The Mighty Ducks," and the little known but wonderful movie "The History of Long Underwear."

• If you go outside and find that your even-side-of-the-street car has been towed to the city impound lot, don't let it get you down. Remember that standing in line gives you the opportunity to meet and greet new friends and neighbors while at the same time learning some new descriptive words about the heritage of the people who run the city. And don't think of it as paying an obscenely large fine, think of it as an opportunity to send a tow truck owner's child to Harvard or Yale.

• A dead car battery isn't such a nuisance when you realize that you are about to expand your knowledge of local facts by discovering just how many other people in the Twin Cities also belong to AAA. Imagine how nice it will be to have that number available the next time you play bar (or coffee-house) trivia.

• Many see cabin fever as a confining time when your family gets on your nerves and the walls start to close in. A time when your mind starts to play tricks on you like making you believe that this would be a good time to start building a bomb shelter in your attic. But, when you look for the silver lining, you find that cabin fever can be a chance for you to grow as a person. After a short confinement you may be surprised to see how close you have become to your spouse (or significant other), your children, your pets, your couch, your remote control, and that ugly robe you've been wearing since Nixon was in office.

• The next time we have measurable precipitation around a foot deep, don't be a gloomy gust of wind. A good blizzard can make you laugh at all those ads for exercise machines. After all, who needs NordicTrack when in your garage you already have NordicShovel. Months of shoveling, plowing and blowing snow – not to mention ice chopping – will really firm up those muscles. Why that's not a snow drift in front of you, it's really a big white mound of opportunity beckoning you to tone up.

And if nothing else can cheer you up during these tropically challenged months remember this: Under all that snow lie a lot of dead mosquitoes.

It Can Never Get Too Cold

Chapter 3

The Other Seasons

The old joke is Minnesota has two seasons – winter and road construction. Of course now they do road construction all year round so that would leave us with one season. But in truth Minnesota has some very nice other seasons. Fall is my favorite even if it comes right before winter. Spring is always a question mark. But come summer, when it is nice, people feel guilty about staying indoors. When I was growing up people would even sleep outdoors – sometimes just for fun whether in a tent in the backyard or sometimes because it was cooler on the screen porch. And, of course, there are those folks who go away each week to their summer cabin or go camping (tent or trailer). We always feel that we "deserve" a nice summer because we lived through winter.

Even so, we complain about summer, spring, and fall too. I think we just want to complain. It bonds us with each other without forcing us to share feelings, names, or bodily fluids. Weather is a big part of Minnesotan life.

A Minnesota Malady:
Fair Weather Madness

It's been a long cold winter followed by a long chilly spring. So it's no wonder that once the temperature was above 40 degrees the roads were overrun with motorcycles, convertibles, bicycles and construction workers.

Twin Cities residents were quick to trade their down jackets for denim jackets and their sweatshirts for t-shirts (except for the dedicated fans of baseball and soccer who were back in their parkas and mittens to watch their kids play ball).

Yes, it is great to have warm weather, but there is the chance that you or someone you love may have WWD (warm weather disorder). Like a compulsive gambler, eater, shopper, or beanie baby buyer, people can spend all their energy trying to get high on warmth. Seek immediate help if you hear yourself or someone close to you saying things like:

• "I've got an idea, let's invite our friends over for an All-You-Can-Eat-Mosquito Barbecue."

• "Today I think I'll just hang around the Twins' stadium and see if there's going to be another tribute to Kirby Puckett."

• "I'm thinking of redecorating the garden shed with a classic art deco look."

• "I love to go down to the freeway with a good book, a blanket, a glass of iced tea, and watch the construction."

- "Gee, the geese at Lake of the Isles sound just like Bea Arthur. I love Bea Arthur."

- "Wow, I never knew how much fun nude badminton could be."

- "I can never get enough of leftover catfish stew."

- "You know, Barney down the street looks pretty good in plaid shorts and black socks."

- "Call the neighbors and see if their dog can come over and dig up our yard."

- "I'm heading over to Uptown to see if I can get a tattoo of Bud Grant."

- "I think I'll see if Rogaine will work on my chest."

- "I'm getting a little tired of all these beautiful sunsets."

- "Let's call and invite your mother to go on vacation with us."

- "Mosquitoes are our friends."

- "Hey, drop that minnow. I'm waiting for word from the government on its appeal."

- "It's not fair; you got to clean up after the neighbor's dog last time. Now it's my turn."

- "At first I thought it was biting me, but now I think that mud turtle is just trying to show it cares."

- "You know, you don't buy Kool-Aid®. You only rent it."

- "Gee Monica, I'm sure glad your kid brought his tuba to the beach."

- "Not tonight, I have a tan line."

- "Let's have a lemonade stand and send the profits to the "Save The CEOs Foundation."

- "Let's go drive around the lakes and blast NPR on our radio."

- "I know it's quite a drive, but how can we miss the Tom Arnold film festival at the Superior Drive-In!"

- "It's so nice to sleep with the windows open so you can wake up smelling the gas fumes from the planes flying over."

- "I won't rest until there is a geranium in every pot and a riding mower in every garage."

For more information call Warm Weather Anonymous, where recovery is taken one degree at a time.

'Tis the Season – For Funnel Romance

If spring is a time when young minds turn to love, then spring is a time when meteorologists' hearts turn to funnel clouds.

Yes, it's that dreadful time of the year – tornado and thunder storm season. And it's not just the potential weather that I have to worry about; it is the dreadful weather reports I have to endure.

I miss Bud Kraehling. He used to stand in front of a board with a magic marker and simply tell us whether it was going to rain or snow and how hot or cold it would probably get. He never tried to scare us. When Bud told us it was time to go to the basement, we all went to the basement.

One year during tornado season I stopped in to see my mom, who was trying to watch a golf tournament. You couldn't really tell if the ball had gone into the hole, because there was this weather report running along the bottom of the screen. To the side of it was a map of Minnesota and Wisconsin that covered about a quarter of the screen. The weather report was like those magicians who keep pulling a handkerchief from their pocket – it went on and on. It not only told you what counties were affected but went on to name every city in each county.

I expected it would soon start to list the names of the families who lived in the cities. At any minute I thought I might see: "This warning is in effect for the Mary Hirsch household in Southwest Minneapolis." It took me less time to read "War and Peace" than to read this weather report.

It Can Never Get Too Cold

But it wasn't enough to have every city and county dance across the screen; we were now being informed about what to do in case of severe weather. Come on, unless someone just moved here from the innermost regions of the rain forest where the last newspaper headline read "Lincoln Elected," they know what to do if there is a storm. And if a storm is coming, should we sit around the living room reading instructions, or should we turn off the television and head to the basement? I think it would be more effective to say nothing about pending storms until the last minute and then just flash a big sign on the television screen that says: "Hey! Get your butt to the basement or kiss it goodbye!"

One year on a Friday night all three of the local channels had interrupted their regular programming for a special "Storm Watch." It was interesting for about three minutes, and then the news teams started to struggle with breaking news that just wasn't breaking. That was when it became amusing.

They provided a lecture on how a storm occurs in nature that sounded a lot like my 5th grade gym teacher trying to explain the wonderful thing that was going to be happening soon to my body. Of course, a storm rarely lasts for three decades and ends with hot flashes, but that's another story.

My favorite moment was when a reporter flying above the storm in a news helicopter told the meteorologist that he was coming back with sensational film of the storm. The meteorologist, obviously not comfortable with winging-it, told us we wouldn't be able to see the film until the reporter got back to the studio, and he wouldn't get back to the studio until the helicopter landed. That was quite a disappointment to those of us who thought he would sky dive into the studio and deliver the film personally.

I'm ready for this year's storm season. I have my candles, my portable radio, and a weather predictor as accurate as anything I've seen lately on television –my Magic 8 Ball.

Watch for the Telltale Markers of Fall

The schools are back in session, the politicians are out in force, and L.L. Bean packages are being delivered in record numbers.

Yes, fall is in the air. And here in Minneapolis there are definite signs of the season:

- Health insurance companies scramble for new reasons not to pay for flu shots.

- The Governor sends in National Guard troops to serve as school patrols.

- Kids are depressed; parents are ecstatic; and teachers can tell you how many more days until June.

- As frost alerts draw closer, local gardeners scramble to find decent-looking sheets they can use to cover their plants and not offend their neighbors.

- Hot chocolate becomes the ammunition of choice for super soakers.

- There are fewer complaints about indoor football and more complaints about outdoor baseball.

- People hang turtlenecks and sweatshirts on their unused exercise equipment instead of beach towels and wet swimsuits.

- Department stores have a rush of people returning the bathing suits they never lost enough weight to get into.

• Homeowners who never took down their Christmas lights now refer to this as an example of their foresight and organizational skill.

• Stores experience a swift decline in the sales of unwanted hair removal products.

• The distinct "swish-swish" of corduroy pants fills the air.

• The only tan lines left are in finer clothing stores.

• The phrase "Going to the cabin" is replaced by "Going to school conferences" as the most frequent excuse to leave work early.

• Local electric companies brace for the Sunday football broadcast power surge.

• A large number of ducks seek sanctuary at area lakes and quack mockingly at hunters who pass by them.

• Florida license plates are now absent from our highways.

• As jack-o-lanterns begin to be carved, families and friends are divided into two camps: those who like the feel of pumpkin seeds in their hands and those who think it has all the appeal of living below clog-dancing elephants.

• The scent of wool is in the air.

• Large amounts of apples and carrots are bought by parents who believe this is the year their children will actually eat what is packed in their school lunch.

• "Christmas starts earlier every year" replaces "Hot enough for you?" as the most popular department store small talk.

• Parents can be heard trying to trick their kids into raking by bribing them with plastic pumpkin bags to fill with leaves.

• "Cuddling by the fireplace" replaces "long walks around the lake" as the number one line on dating sites.

• The ratio of Minnesotans to turtlenecks rises to 1:6.

• Sweaters that were only seen during the summer on infomercials are now appearing at coffee and bagel shops all over town.

• Certain politicans and their staff are anxiously antici-pating the days when "I was trying to get out of the cold" will be an acceptable reason for stepping into "gentlemen's clubs" for a cup of coffee.

You Know It's Spring When...

Meteorologists may tell you that spring starts March 21, but in Minneapolis we don't need a calendar to tell us when spring starts – we can recognize the signs:

• Seeing the first robin droppings on your car.

• Awakening Sunday morning to the almost forgotten song of your neighbor revving up the power lawn mower.

• Cranking up your television and radio so you can hear them over the sound of airplanes flying overhead.

• Experiencing that tickling sensation as a gnat flies up your nose.

• Seeing your neighbor, the CPA, during the daylight for the first time in four months.

• Discovering that you still can't fit into the clothes you couldn't fit into last spring but that you saved to wear this spring because you were really going to lose weight over the winter.

• Being asked at least daily to sponsor someone in a walk/run/jog/skate-a-thon.

• Seeing signs of new life and eternal hope return to the faces of your kids' teachers.

• Experiencing a sudden craving for a Dilly Bar.

• Realizing that the air elves did not pop in during the

winter and inflate the tires on your bike.

• Seeing the neighbor down the block who you were about to report missing to the police.

• Hearing the strains of the new songs your neighbor's son has learned on the violin during the school year.

• The previous year car clearance sale ads finally disappear from the television and radio.

• "Wind Chill Factor" is once again a movie and book.

• Arriving home with your first garage sale purchase.

• The sounds of the couple across the street having their first fight about fishing weekends.

• You put a hold on your career search in Phoenix.

• Someone has written "Wash Me" in the dirt on your car.

• You can listen to the weather report without having a hotline counselor standing by.

Consider, Again, the Homely
Pothole...

Like everyone else in Minneapolis, I have spent a great deal of energy complaining about, and circumventing, the potholes that have taken over our city.

I like to think of pothole-bashing as a transitional period of complaining that falls between "Cold enough for ya" and "Hot enough for ya."

Driving through the city, I have discovered it is wise not to leave the house without first emptying my bladder. And when I am bouncing about on the bus, I see that my fellow passengers and I look like Metro Transit bobbleheads.

I used to think it was impossible to find anything positive in a pothole (although I still believe it is possible we may find Jimmy Hoffa in one someday). But that changed this winter when I discovered that every pothole has its silver lining.

While waiting for a bus I saw a minivan take a dive into the local corner crater. While that wasn't interesting, or even funny, in itself, I also watched the stunned motorist lose a grip on his cellular phone and saw it go sailing into the back seat. Now that was funny.

That got me to thinking that perhaps some good can come from potholes after all.

First, I think we need to change the name. Yes, a pothole by any other name would sink as deep, but names can also fuel irritation.

For example, why not stop thinking of them as potholes but rather as GIAs – Geologically Impaired Areas. Doesn't that sound nicer already? You immediately want to have fundraisers for the geologically impaired, but selling a ticket to the Pothole Gala Ball could be a hard sell. A simple name change could make a big difference.

Next, we need to remember that it takes a village to raise a pothole, so why not start a program called "Adopt a Pothole." Imagine driving down the street and seeing signs to the left of you and signs to the right of you saying "You Betcha, This Pothole Has Been Adopted by The Sons of Norway Then," or "You Are Approaching The GIA Formerly Known As Pothole That Has Been Adopted By The Fan Club Of The Artist Formerly Known As Prince," or "This Geologically Impaired Area Adopted (And Available At A Good Price) By Smith Realty."

And how about some creative uses for these GIAs? We could string nine or 18 of them together as a golf course and create the Concrete County Club.

Potholes can play an important role in the future by becoming the great equalizer in our society. A pothole doesn't care what race you are, how much money you have, what your religious beliefs may be, or whether or not you would want to date Ellen Degeneres; it is an equal opportunity menace.

And why not use them to improve our city's quality of life. Plant a geranium, some tulips, a tree or two in the potholes of your street. Stock them with walleye and host the fishing opener on Excelsior Boulevard. Move the Aquatennial regatta from Lake Harriet to Lake Harriet Parkway. Throw pennies in and make a wish. Invite Martha Stewart to tape a special here: "Now This Is Pothole Living."

Don't forget: where there is an abundance of potholes, there is never a need to purchase a new hub cap for your car. Eventually one or two will roll into your yard, and you can just slap them on your car and head on out.

For myself, I think I will seize the opportunity these craters have presented and write a screenplay about how the pothole is a symbol of humankind's struggle against the holes of our soul and sell it to the Coen brothers.

Lake Cabin Fever

This summer, you'll know you've been at the lake cabin too long when you hear yourself say:

• "Wow, that was fun – now you pick the leeches off of me."

• "You've seen one beautiful sunset, you've seen them all."

• "Let's invite your mother to stay with us up here for a month or two."

• "Bats are our friends."

• "It's no fair – you got to clean the septic tank last time."

• "Oh good, a rainy day – we can play another game of Candyland."

• "Gee, Charlie, I'm sure glad your kid brought his accordion with him."

• "Not tonight – I want to listen to the crickets chirp."

Mary E. Hirsch

Chapter 4

HOLIDAYS IN MINNESOTA

Oh sure you may think Minnesota has the same holidays as everyone else ... but when was the last time there was a big Svenskarnas Dag celebration in Memphis? And although we may celebrate the same day as shown on the calendar how many people outside of Minnesota eat lefse, lutefisk, and liver knadle soup – on purpose – at Christmas? Do you think moms in Miami buy Halloween costumes that will fit over ski jackets and snow pants? Have you ever hunted for an Easter egg in a 2-foot snow drift or had your Christmas parade cancelled because the band players lips would freeze to their instruments if they march?

Welcome to the holidays in Minnesota.

CHRISTMAS

Caring Carols

In recognition of "Minnesota Nice," we provide you with politically correct titles for traditional carols in hopes that no one will be offended this holiday season. (The offensive titles can be found on the next page.)

1. I'm Envisioning a Culturally Diverse December 25th With a Covering of Crystallized Water Particles of Non-color

2. Noise Pollution-Free Evening, Spiritually Empowered Evening

3. Oh Botanical Growth With Special Meaning Attributed to December 25th

4. This Unit of Royal Males Coming from Eastern Geographic Locations

5. Higher Power (of your understanding) Grant Serenity to You Jocular Males of Distinguishable Breeding

6. Deprivation of Sadness to the Conglomerate of Nations Found on this Biosphere

7. Actively Listen! The Communicating Spirit Guides of Heaven are Doing Music

8. Oh Small Community of the Middle East

9. Temporarily Relocated in Alternative Housing Shared with Nondomesticated Animal Companions

10. Recognized Catholic Icon Named Nicholas Who Is a Euphoric Senior Citizen

1. I'm Dreaming of a White Christmas

2. Silent Night, Holy Night

3. Oh Christmas Tree

4. We Three Kings of Orient Are

5. God Rest Ye Merry Gentlemen

6. Joy to the World

7. Hark! The Herald Angels Sing

8. Oh Little Town of Bethlehem

9. Away in a Manger

10. Jolly Old St. Nicholas

T'was The Night Before Christmas ...
Minneapolis Style

T'was the night before Christmas and all 'round the lakes,
The folks weren't aware of the fast-falling flakes.
The only noise to fill the night air,
Were planes filled with people heading elsewhere.

The ducks, geese and ganders were snug in their nests,
There was a holiday stillness in the city's Southwest.
And I in my long johns – not quite Maidenform,
Was under my blanket trying to get warm.

When out on the street there arose such a clatter,
So loud I could barely hear my teeth chatter.
Away to the window I trudged like a slug,
One look outside and I grunted "Humbug!"

The street lights illumined four new feet of snow,
"Hey, tomorrow is Christmas; we've places to go!"
But what was that noise that from my bed did arouse?
It's the city's fleet of eight shiny snow plows!

With eight little drivers whose faces did shine,
'Cause they knew they were all getting paid double time.
Pressured to be done by break of day.
They shifted their gears and were underway.

To Washburn, to Vincent, to Blaisdell, Dupont,
To Pleasant, to Thomas, to Morgan, Fremont.
To the top of the hills, to the streets down below,
Plow away, plow away, plow away snow.

Mary E. Hirsch

So up and down streets the snow plows did rumble,
As the walls of fresh snow started to crumble,
And then with a scraping I saw down the road,
City sand trucks sprinkling their load.

They kept at their task – they didn't stop work,
With those kind of wages who would but a jerk?
They pushed and they plowed
And they plowed and they pushed,
The engines were humming, the drivers were bushed.

And when the fresh snow gave way to cement,
They lifted their plows – to the next street they went.
But I heard them exclaim as they drove through the ice thicket,
"Move your damn car or we'll give you a ticket."

HALLOWEEN

Minnesota Horror Stories

In the spirit of a good old-fashioned Minnesota Halloween, here are some bone-chillers we'd like to see on Netflix:

- The Svensens think it's going to be just another night of rosmaling when suddenly their youngest, Inga, starts delivering old gubernatorial addresses. It's **A Nightmare on Elmer Anderson Street.**

- Poor Mel. He thought he'd invested in a small-town meat packing plant. Little did he know he'd bought a piece of **The Spamityville Horror.**

- They're punk. They're pierced. They're **The Creatures From Hennepin and Lagoon.**

- Awakened by warm spring temperatures, a strange race of manlike monsters brutalizes local motorists. They get what's coming to them, though, in **Godzilla Versus MnDOT.** Caution: This road is under destruction.

The Bride of Frankensven

If you see a ghost or a goblin this Halloween, give it a break – maybe even a nice treat – because it's no easy trick being a ghoul in Minnesota. Here are some of the biggest complaints of our state's supernatural residents:

• Can't tell when Scandinavians are scared. It's not like their faces can get paler.

• Every time you want to haunt some church basement, it's filled with people who want to give you a group hug.

• Try to send a chill up the spine of a guy who's just spent an hour shoveling out his car in a wind chill of 50 below.

• Hard to live with new-age snobbery – angels good; ghosts bad!

• So many lakes, so few drowned sailors to go around.

• Can't be seen in a blizzard without a red plaid hat.

• Can't hear yourself moan, wail, or shriek above the noise of low-flying airplanes.

• How can you be nasty to people who keep saying, "Have a nice day"?

• The humidity makes everyone feel clammy.

• Just looking at Spam makes our blood run warm.

- Every winter it's the same thing: haunted cabin fever.

- Try to come up with a face scarier than Jessie Ventura.

- The Department of Supernatural Resources keeps raising the price of haunting licenses.

- Lutherans refuse to have the hell scared out of them.

Headlines in Minnesota Hell

The day starts like any other. You open your front door, pick up the morning paper, read the headlines, and suddenly – you're in Minnesota Hell:

• Twins starting pitcher will be Barry Manilow

• It's "Hug a Politician" month

• Mosquitoes declared endangered species – now it's the law: no mosquito-swatting

• MPR to unveil new disco format

• Office of Tourism: We can find only 9,999 lakes

• FDA says beer decreases testosterone levels in men

• Northern lights declared hoax – lightning bug cult suspected

• Aliens abduct Minnesota Legislature -- Promise To Return Them In Time For Elections

• Newest treat: Spam-sicles

• Mississippi reverses flow – Cajun polka is born

• Viking Stadium astroturf missing – savage Chia pets sought

Are There Ghosts In The 'Hood?

We've all read stories that scared us: "Frankenstein," "Cujo," "The Bridges of Madison County."

But how do we know we aren't part of such supernatural occurrences? This Halloween watch for the following signs. If they occur, there is a good chance your house is haunted.

- Cheeez Whiz has become your favorite food.

- Every time you open you refrigerator, you hear "Lady of Spain" on the accordion.

- The afghan you've been crocheting just had puppies.

- A "Don't Blame Me, I Voted for Nixon" bumper sticker keeps appearing on your car.

- You've begun translating the works of Garrison Keillor into Klingon.

- You realize John Dillinger is still sleeping here.

- Your walls are covered with milfoil.

- You refuse to leave the house unless you are wearing a blowing shirt with the name "Bud" on it.

- Every channel on your television set broadcasts the meeting of the Hennepin County Board of Commissioners.

- Your pajamas have feet in them – and they aren't yours.

- There's a voice coming from your dishwasher saying "Bring me the head of the Maytag Repairman."

- You swear you see the profile of Hubert Humphrey in your baked potato.

- All your underwear is turned inside out, while you're wearing it.

- Late at night you can see Bert Parks wandering the halls wearing a one-piece Jantzen swimsuit and 4-inch heels.

- There's a plaid form floating through the air saying "Yah, sure, you BOOOOtcha."

- No matter how hard you try, every pumpkin you carve looks like Walter Mondale.

- "Tour Iowa" brochures keep appearing your mailbox.

- You are starting to believe that the Vikings will win the Super Bowl.

- Your Barcalounger does.

- The squirrels on your windowsill are reciting poems by Robert Bly.

- There are skeletons in your closet, and you aren't even running for public office.

- Your children are saying words like "OK" and "Please," and their rooms are picked up.

- Stephen King just delivered a pizza – and you didn't order one.

But the most conclusive sign that your house is haunted will be if you discover your entire family is looking forward to the next presidential elections.

APRIL FOOL'S DAY

Minnesota Fools

This April Fool's Day, remember, you can fool some of the people all of the time, and all of the people some of the time – but there are no fools quite like these Minnesota fools:

- People who subscribed to cable just to watch government meetings.

- The woman who bought a mattress when it wasn't on sale.

- The angler who picked the spot for his icehouse based on the quality of the public schools in the area.

- Anyone who bought Thirst Alert – a product that detects when a person needs a beer.

- The student who enrolled at the University of Minnesota for its great football program and small-town atmosphere.

- The producer who financed the filming of *Lethargic Loons*, the story of a group of upbeat, fun-loving kids brought down by a lacrosse coach getting in touch with his inner child.

- The guy who checked into Hazelden because he thought it was a pro golf school.

- The guy who sold his snowblower in March because winter was over.

- The artist who asked for the booth right next to the mini-donut truck at the art fair.

- The Minnesota legislator who decided to go on a trip sponsored by a lobbyist – right before network sweeps month.

Mary E. Hirsch

NATIONAL ANTI-BOREDOM MONTH

31 Ways To Perk Up National Anti-Boredom Month

Did you know July is National Anti-Boredom Month? Well, it is. It is also Hitchhiking Month, National Hot Dog Month, National Ice Cream Month, National Recreation and Park Month, and National Picnic Month. It would seem to me if you simply celebrated the other National Month events, there would be no need for a National Anti-Boredom Month, but I have a feeling it came about for two reason. First, July is the time when parents are getting sick of hearing their kids say, "There's nothing to do: I'm bored." Second, adults are also becoming bored now that the simple thrill of being outside without seeing your breath is wearing off.

There are plenty of articles and books with ideas for keeping kids busy. (These are in addition to the standard parent suggestions: call a friend, read a book, clean your room, change your socks, become a highly skilled athlete who will make millions of dollars someday). But, there are few ideas given to adults who are starting to get patio fever. So, in honor of National Anti-Boredom Month, here are 31 suggestions of things to do in July to keep from being bored.

- July 1: Drive around Bde Maka Ska (fna Lake Calhoun) with polka music cranked up on your car stereo. If harassed, yell "Whoopee John Reigns!"

- July 2: Hold a garage sale and sell only used underwear and half-eaten fruit, then observe shoppers' reactions. For extra excitement, create an interpretive dance based on these reactions and then apply for a grant from the Minnesota Arts Board to fund your work.

- July 3: Put a red silk cape on your dog, take it for a walk at the park, and when it makes a deposit in the grass, refuse to pick it up, claiming that the grass is now possessed with super growing powers.

- July 4: Learn to play all of the marches of John Philip Sousa on your armpits and then invite your relatives over for an Independence Day concert.

- July 5: Attend the annual picnic of the National Rifle Association and at the end of the day suggest that everyone get together for a group hug and to sing "Blowing In The Wind."

- July 6: Organize a block party based on the theme "I'm Okay: You're Getting On My Nerves."

- July 7: Host a "Robert Bly Unplugged" concert at the Lake Harriet Bandshell.

- July 8: Float down Minnehaha Creek singing the score of "Showboat."

- July 9: Begin preparing for the Twin Cities Marathon by picking out the spot along the route where you are going to sit and watch the runners go by.

- July 10: Start a new charity to buy sunscreen for Scandianvians -- call it Save The Pales.

- July 11: Become active in lobbying the city council for a cellulite mandatory beach.

- July 12: Rearrange your vegetable garden in alphabetical order.

- July 13: Take a Malibu Barbie doll to the beach and watch her pick up hunks.

- July 14: Have a Margarita stand on the corner of your block.

- July 15: Sit in the waiting room of the Department of Motor Vehicles wearing a T-shirt saying "I Love Road Construction," then journal about the responses you trigger.

- July 16: Crochet a compost bin cozy.

- July 17: Stand outside the restrooms at Target Field and sing "Let It Go" when people enter.

- July 18: Create a Minnesota Fringe Festival show combining slam poetry with fish cleaning -- in the nude.

- July 19: Loiter at the Lake Harriet water pump and engage visitors in a debate over the works of Kafka as metaphor for bocche ball.

- July 20: Organize a community choir that visits the fishing and boating docks of local lakes and sings sea chanteys.

- July 21: Walk your Chia pet around Lake of the Isles.

- July 22: Give public readings of your latest poetry at park tennis courts.

- July 23: Sculpt your hedges to look like local TV meteorologists.

- July 24: Make yourself a costume out of seaweed and start a new career as Milfoil Man.

- July 25: Name all the ducks at Lake Harriet after famous figures in maritime history.

- July 26: Drive down Hennepin Avenue at 5 mph and jot down all the sentiments expressed by other drivers, then write a one-act play based on this experience.

- July 27: Organize a picnic in the park around the theme "What's All This Fuss About Cholesterol – Fix Me Another Brat."

- July 28: Do a load of laundry and instead of using the dryer hang your clothese out to dry --- on the light rail.

- July 29: Learn how to mime in a foreign language.

- July 30: Build a backyard gazebo out of Legos.

- July 31: Hang out at the archery range on William Berry Road wearing green tights and ask passer-bys if they want to be part of your "Merry Band."

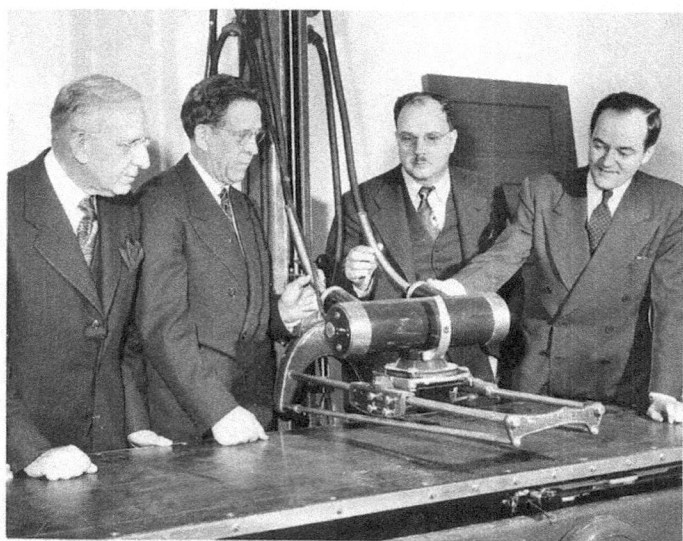

Chapter 5

MINNESOTA POLITICS

If you were to look at the Presidential elections it would be obvious that Minnesota is full of runner-ups or almost candidates. Humphrey, Mondale, McCarthy, and of course Harold Stassen who started running for President when Andrew Jackson was the nominee. Two people from Minnesota recently ran for President -- former Governor Tim Pawlenty and former Representative Michele Bachmann. I am thinking of tossing my hat into the ring too just so we can have three unqualified people from Minnesota running for President.

But we also have some interesting politics here -- from flavored milk stand owner to the Senate Rudy Boschwitz; from Saturday Night Live writer/performer to the Senate Al Franken; and from the World Wrestling Federation to Governor Jesse Ventura. And of course we have the celebrity stall in the airport men's room where a certain former Senator was caught in a compromising position. We are fly over country not fly open country.

So here are some columns where I discuss Minnesota Politics and what they mean to me.

A Question to Keep You Awake at Night:
What Does the Lieutenant Governor Do?

Well, it's official – As of Aug. 1 a law went into effect confirming that if the Governor is unable to fulfill his or her duties, the Lieutenant Governor will take over. I'll sleep better knowing that we won't have to be without someone to fight with the opposition, appear at public functionss, or fail to catch a fish on the opening weekend of fishing season.

But who the heck is going to take over the Lieutenant Governor's duties? Few people are aware of the magnitude of duties he or she must perform. A few of these obligations include:

• Swatting the first mosquito of the season.

• Making sure no pieces are missing from the jigsaw puzzles in the Governor's mansion.

• Learning all the words to "Hail Minnesota" and be ready to sing it when asked.

• Performing shadow puppets at the Mansion Talent Show.

• Telling visitors at the mansion to stay off the grass.

• Checking the governor's boat for milfoil at the fishing opener.

• Steaming uncancelled stamps off tax return envelopes.

• Making tardy legislators stay after session and clean the blackboards.

• Kicking the butt of the other 49 lieutenant governors in the annual "Bobbing for Apples" competition.

• Fixing overdue library book fines for governor's staff members.

• Making sure the Lambada is not danced at any state functions.

• Tossing out the first stick at the opening of whittling season.

• Returning the state's Publisher's Clearninghouse Sweepstakes entry.

• Keeping the Gopher 5 balls clean and shiny.

• Buying toilet paper for tee-peeing political opponents' houses on election night.

• Bringing coleslaw to Legislature potlucks.

• Decorating the gym for the Inauguration Ball.

• Being artistic director for the MnDOT Gregorian Chant Choral Society.

Got Your Ole and Lena License?

Legislators typically turn to licenses or taxes on cigarettes, liquor and gasoline to produce revenue. But should we all become nonsmoking, teetotaling car poolers, here's a look at other vices Minnesota could either tax, fine or require a permit for.

- Taking up more than one parking spot (double fine for winter).

- Ole and Lena joke books.

- Long underwear.

- Imported beer (from any of the other 49 states).

- Wearing too much perfume.

- Sidewalk salt.

- Crossing the state border.

- Using the word "consultant" on your business cards.

- Looking at Garrison Keillor if you see him on the street.

- Playing in a polka band.

- Checking out more than 10 items in an express lane.

- Displaying a bumper sticker that says you "heart" anything.

- Self-help books.

- Following public officials with a camera (plus a "Sweeps Month" surcharge).

- Having an answering-machine message longer than 10 seconds.

Little-Known State Laws Adopted By This Year's Legislature

The Minnesota Legislature has been busy.

While battles over matters such as health care, crime prevention, property taxes, bond issues, airport location, school testing, etc. have been in the headlines, some very important new laws may have slipped by Minnesotans unnoticed.

So as a public service, here are a few laws that may be of special interest to local residents:

- No one over the age of 105 can tap dance nude on the docks of Lake Harriet.

- Public school teachers cannot punish children by making them learn all the words to "Mandy."

- Our new state motto is "Cold Enough For Ya?"

- Restaurants cannot discriminate against customers based on bad hair.

- Police officers may not imitate Elmer Fudd while reading a suspect his Miranda rights. However, they are allowed to say "I got you now, you wascally wobber."

- Cars abandoned in a pothole for over 24 hours become the property of the State Department of Transportation.

- Accordions in a boat do not count as flotation devices.

- There must be at least one pretentious person sitting outside a coffee shop at all times—weather permitting.

- Nursing homes may not force residents to participate in arts and crafts or to do the Hokey Pokey.

- Lonely bachelor farmers may not declare their livestock as dependents.

- No one can borrow "The Bridges of Madison County" more than once from a library without taking an MMPI test.

- Conga lines may use the sane lane but must stay to the right so faster traffic can pass.

- In an effort to refrain from using derogatory words, the "odd" side of the street will now be referred to as "the side of the street that cannot be evenly divided by two."

- Sidewalks must be shoveled right after a snow storm or a visit by a political candidate.

- You may not hum "Unchained Melody" while participating in a pottery class.

- You cannot fire someone for not knowing all the words to "Hail Minnesota."

- You may not wear black socks and sandals at a public beach unless accompanied by a metal detector.

- You must be 21 years of age or older to drink Lutefisk wine.

It Can Never Get Too Cold

- Local cable stations may not carry more than 43 city meeting channels.

- It's a misdemeanor to recite dirty poems while rollerblading around Lake of the Isles.

- Parents who are delinquent in child support can be denied a fishing license and beer.

- Plaid flannel is now the state fabric.

- Lutherans do not have to smile for a picture ID.

And, most importantly, although we've always known it, it's now the law: Heat good; humidity bad.

Pay Up For Major-League Humor

The Twins demanded that a new outdoor stadium be built for them. They wanted a large part of that stadium to be paid for by Minnesota taxpayers. If they didn't get the stadium, the team's management strongly hinted that they may leave the Twin Cities. And, as we know, they got it -- Target Field.

Well, I've been in the Twin Cities longer than the Twins, and I have a few demands of my own. Demands that, if not met by the City Council or Legislature, may cause me to leave the Twin Cities:

- I must be crowned Aquatennial Queen and have my face carved out of butter. (I know that's Princess Kay of the Milky Way, but I don't want to be a princess: I want to be a queen, and I want my face carved out of butter.)

- No dogs in the Twin Cities can be named Fifi, Poopsie or Waggles.

- Bagel shops must agree to sell glazed donuts.

- The City must institute a law that limits each citizen to having only four body parts pierced.

- Keiffer Sutherland's birthday (December 21) must be declared a national holiday.

- Anyone who is caught riding their bike in the winter must be immediately placed into counseling.

- No one can serve on the Metropolitan Airports Commission unless they live on the airport flight path.

It Can Never Get Too Cold

- All traffic cops must know how to do the Macarena.

- News anchors can only wear glasses on the air if they file an optometrist's affidavit with the FCC proving that they need to wear glasses.

- When the President visits the Twin Cities, his motorcade cannot be on the streets during rush hour.

- The next time the Governor closes all the schools he must let any parent leave their kids at his mansion for the day.

- Every pothole must be repaired by April 30.

- It should be a felony to rollerblade around the lake while talking on a cellular phone.

- No television station can continue to have its severe weather reports written by Stephen King.

- The bottoms of all low-flying planes must be painted with funny pictures of legislators.

- Severe weather reports (including multicolored maps) cannot take up more than 10 percent of the television screen, unless they are being broadcast during a Hallmark made-for-TV movie.

- From now on I want to be called "The Goddess Formerly Known As Mary."

So, those are my demands. If not met, I may be packing up my computer and heading to some other city; some place exotic like Honolulu, Hilton Head or Hastings.

Raw Poll

There are, of course, many ways to greet politicians who appear at your door. The strategies below might help when they come knocking at your door this fall.

- Announce, "You're late!" and demand a free pizza.

- Ask the candidate where he or she will be spending eternity.

- Issue an invitation to your next Tap Dancers for a Clothing-Optional Society meeting.

- Find out where the candidate stands on making elbow macaroni the official state pasta.

- Ask the candidate to watch your kids for a few hours while you go to your ceramics class.

- Mention that you're looking for someone to sponsor a bill making it illegal for an FM radio station to play anything by the Captain and Tenille.

- Explain that you refuse to vote until Pee-Wee Herman is granted clemency.

- Frantically explain that someone just ran over your cat but that you'd be glad to discuss politics while you scrape Fluffy off the pavement.

- Insist that before you can commit your vote to any candidate, you must discuss your options with Elvis.

Sponsorships Can Cure the
McCity's Finanacil McIlls

The City of Minneapolis changed the name of the Hubert Humphrey Metrodome to the Mall of America Metrodome. The new stadium is the U.S. Bank Stadium. This is not a reflection on the late vice president, but rather is an economic decision. Apparently companies will pay big bucks to plaster their name on a sports arena – the Target Center and Target Field being a local example.

At a time when Minneapolis is in great need of money this seems to be a better answer than trying to collect money at the lakes parking lots. But why stop at sports arenas? Think of all the money that could be made by selling the city off a piece at a time.

Now there are some obvious places where a sponsor would be appropriate. For example, we could have the Gatorade Energy Center, the Ivory Snow Removal Department, and the Hazelden Treatment Plant.

Cigarette companies are always looking for new ways to promote their products. Imagine the thrill of seeing smoke pour out of the Marlboro Incinerator or having your son or daughter attend Camel High, play ball at Salem Park, or find a book at Winston Library. Of course, all these facilities would come with a warning from the Surgeon General.

When downtown, you could see the golden arches in front of Ronald McDonald City Hall, which would house our McGovernment. ("Would you like fries with your tax assessment?") Emergency calls to 911 would hear the following message: "While you're waiting for that emergency vehicle to arrive, wouldn't this be a good time for a big dish of Kemp's

Ice Cream?"

We could paint the Lake Harriet Bandstand yellow and blue and rename it the Best Buy Bandstand. And speaking of Lake Harriet, who is Harriet and what has she done for us lately? Wouldn't it be nice to take a stroll around Lake Medtronic or ride the 'CCO Trolley?

Those vintage bathrooms would be restored quickly when named the Pillsbury Potties, with facilities for Doughboys and Doughgirls. In fact, just renaming lakes alone could pay for city services. It's just as easy to fish, swim and walk at Lake Toro, Lake Fruit-of-the-Loom, Lake of the Whopper and Jell-O Lake (with Jiggler Beach being a very popular spot). How about Xcel Falls? For an extra million or two, we'll throw in the creek and the parkway. It certainly wouldn't be any big deal to create Wells Fargo River Road, now would it?

Law enforcement could be funded with the Hefty Zip-Lock Jail, the Coors Detox Center, the Maaco Impound Lot, and the NordicTrack Workout House. Teenagers would feel right at home in The Gap Juvenile Hall, where their uniforms would include an "I Just Didn't Do It" Nike hat – to be worn backwards. Parking tickets would come with valuable coupons for Cub Foods, and everyone pulled over for speeding would receive a two-for-the-price-of-one dinner at Hardees. Those red fire engines would look extra nice sporting a Pennzoil logo, and those firefighter hats would work just as well in a nice John Deere green.

If these sponsorship ideas are implemented, it won't be long before the city will have an excess of funds available.

Now that would make 3M-inneapolis a great place to live.

You Can't Afford To Be In The Dark About These Laws

Recently the Minneapolis City Council decided to permit fully-clothed people to dance until 3 a.m. in certain bars. I have to plead ignorance, because I didn't even know there was a law prohibiting such dancing. (Well, actually, I didn't know there were people who could manage to stay up that late, much less dance.) So I started to wonder what other unique laws I am unaware of. Based on my powers of observation, my keen journalistic mind, and my excessive caffeine consumption, I have come to the conclusion that the city of Minneapolis may have following laws in effect:

- *If you don't clean up after your dog, the city will give your name and address to the local Finnish mafia.

- Bank tellers must say "Have a nice day" or the transaction is void.

- It is illegal to ride an MTC bus while wearing a live skunk on your head.

- White shoes shall not be worn past Labor Day or before Memorial Day (with the exception of a warm, sunny Easter and/or Palm Sunday).

- Every garage sale must have a minimum of three used polka albums, five Readers' Digest condensed books, and a crocheted poodle toilet paper cover.

- If you want to turn right on red, be sure to stop in the crossing area so no pedestrian can get by.

- Smiling at a Lutheran during Lent is grounds for deportation to North Dakota.

- The motto "City of Lakes" was replaced with "Heat good; humidity bad."

- French may not be spoken within two miles of Nicollet Mall.

- A pan of Rice Krispie bars must be present at all potlucks.

- It is illegal to carry a concealed tattoo of Al Franken on your body.

- There is no statute of limitations on adjustments to your water bill.

- A block party must have a minimum of three card tables in order to qualify for street barrier privileges.

- School bus drivers may not punish rowdy kids by forcing them to listen to Whoopee John music.

- Due to a conflict of interest, cat film festivals may not be held on the opening day of fishing.

- No nude clog dancing after 2 a.m. unless accompanied by a visiting Scandinavian dignitary.

- A Justice League membership card is not acceptable ID for cashing a check, although it can be used to register to vote.

- It is a misdemeanor to go door-to-door singing the greatest hits of the Bee Gees.

The Lakes: Dreaming Of What Might Have Been

The great debate in Minneapolis has been the redesigning of the city lakes. The goal was to make the lakes more accessible to people and to improve the quality of the lake environment. Many ideas were offered and a few were chosen.

While change is never easy (or at least that's what all the great philosophers say when they aren't discussing that stupid tree falling in the woods when no one is around), it may help those of you who are having a hard time coming to grips with the impending changes to see what ideas were rejected.

- Get rid of the Rose Garden and open a trailer park.

- Make the lakes more appealing to gamblers. Turn the paddle boat into the Minnesota Lottery's first floating casino.

- To increase revenues and get more people to use the pay parking lots, hire Super Models to serve as attendants. The lots will soon be overflowing with mid-life crises convertibles.

- Make the area more appealing to people who have no desire to walk, run, skate or cycle around the lakes by turning Beard's Pleasance into a Beer's Garden.

- Combine the rock garden with a Spam sculpture garden.

- Dispel the animosity between the citizens and City Hall by installing a Minneapolis City Council Kissing Booth.

- Close the boat launch entirely and have boats dropped into water by airplanes flying overhead.

- Outdoor dining and conversation can flourish if the docks are leased to coffee shops and/or bagel stores.

- Require any jogger found running on the grass to listen to the last 10 State of the City addresses.

- Dogs are welcome at the lake, but they must be on a leash at all times, have a license, and cannot be named Boopsie or Precious.

- To avoid traffic congestion at the Bandshell, the only bands that will be allowed to play are ones that feature Jerry Vale retrospectives or the music of junior high bands.

- Public bathrooms will be closed, but we're sure people living on the lake won't mind if you go up to their door and ask to use their bathroom.

- The tennis courts will be removed and replaced with a Volvo dealership.

- All vegetation in the Bird Sanctuary will be cut down and replaced with the ice house storage facilities.

- To keep people from lingering too long at the beach, the National Guard will serve as lifeguards.

- To alleviate parking problems, picnic areas will be replaced by fast-food franchises with drive-through windows. This will allow people to eat at the lake but not park in the process.

- The trolley cars will also serve as the offices for the Minneapolis Park Board.

- The elf house will be replaced by Elf Village, a shopping center designed to meet all your small needs.

- Turn the lower east road into a drag strip. This will keep traffic moving quickly and avoid gawker slowdowns.

- Create a lane for Class A bikers (faster) on the parkway and Class H bikers (huffin' and puffin') on the current dirt paths.

But I think the proposal that really went too far was the one that suggested changing the name of Lake Harriet to Lake City Council.

It Can Never Get Too Cold

Chapter 6

The Great Outdoors

I once read that there are actually over 15,000 lakes in Minnesota and based on that fact, Minnesota has more shoreline than California, Florida and Hawaii put together. So why doesn't that comfort me in the middle of January?

Of course everyone in the world has outdoors, unless they don't have indoors, in which case they can't have out or doors so they have nothingness and will eventually open a yoga studio. I think these are the same people who are in that forest where the tree falls but they don't hear it because they are trying to figure out if the egg they found was there before the chicken. But I digress.

There is indeed a lot of outdoors in Minnesota and some of it is Great and some of it is okay and some of it just plan sucks. In general we try to keep away from the just plan suck outdoors and go the great outdoors which tends to be found in parks and near water.

If you took all the trouble to suffer through winter, in Minnesota you enjoy the Great Outdoors whenever you get the chance -- even if it just means opening your window at night during "good sleepin' weather. "

Here are some thoughts on the outdoors we call Minnesota.

Minnesota Camping Tips

Every spring and summer Minnesotans head for the wilds, many of them novices of camping. To help these beginning campers avoid some pitfalls, we offer a few tips they won't find in any of the Minnesota Department of Natural Resources brochures:

- Never pound tent stakes with a skunk.

- Don't volunteer to let someone put aluminum siding on your tent as a model for the rest of the campground.

- Don't park your mobile home down-wind from the latrines.

- A Honeywell security system sign outside your tent will do little to keep out raccoons.

- Never camp next to someone whose truck has a sticker saying "I Brake For Convicted Felons."

- Don't feed the bears – they'll never learn to become self-sufficient and will probably only end up becoming burdens to society.

- Don't stay at a campground called Rustic Landfill.

- Best Western is not a national park.

- Don't drink from the water jug of someone named Crusher.

- Angry bears do not respond well to a group hug.

- Beware of camping con artists. Calvin Klein does not make a bug repellent.

- If you spot Elvis at your campground, be sure to store your peach pies in an airtight container and hang them from a tree.

Rationalize That Fishing Addiction!

You can always tell when fishing season has started because infants aren't the only ones at the lake in rubber pants.

I'm always amazed at people who fish. Most of them wouldn't get out of bed before 6 a.m. to see the Pope tap dance on their roof, but taunt them with the thought of sitting in a boat all day with a bucket full of minnows, a warm six-pack and a bag of chips, and they are out the door before sunrise.

Fishing fascinates me. It's one of the only times a person gets to sit for hours and do next to nothing without being elected to public office. When my best friend returned to Minnesota for a visit last summer, her son and daughter fell in love with fishing. In fact, one day they said they'd rather go fishing than to the Mall of America, which is right up there with saying, "I'd rather eat broccoli than a hot fudge sundae," or, "I'd rather do my homework than play Super Nintendo."

Personally, I've only been fishing once. My father took me and my brother fishing when I was around 7 or 8. My father and brother caught zippo, zilch and zero, while I caught three fish. I was never invited again. Of course this may have had nothing to do with my superior fishing skills and a lot to do with the fact that I wouldn't stop talking and attempted to set all the minnows free rather than see them get "the hook."

Fishing season also means the start of some lively "discussions" between couples where one person loves to fish and the other doesn't. (Most often the person who loves to fish is the person with the Y chromosome, but not always.) I've witnessed a few of these discussions, and they are never pretty.

So, if this year you find yourself in a spot where your spouse thinks you are spending a little too much time fishing, perhaps it would be better to say, "I'm not fishing dear, I'm..."

- Hunting down enemy walleye.

- Seeking serenity so I can be a more caring and compassionate person.

- Taking juvenile delinquent minnows on an outing.

- Frolicking with nature.

- Casting my troubles on the waters.

- Doing research for a future Ph.D. dissertation: "Fishing as Metaphor for Social Change."

- Allowing myself to become part of the circle of life – the part that catches, guts, skins and eats fish.

- Trying to overcome my fear of leeches.

- Working on my next book: "Zen and the Art of Fly Casting."

- Meeting Elvis in the middle of the lake to arrange for his return to show biz.

- Making extra money delivering pizzas to fishing boats.

It Can Never Get Too Cold

- Trying to find the tire I lost from my '76 Pinto.

- Looking for Jimmy Hoffa.

- Part of a government test on how long a six pack of beer can stay cold in a cooler on a fishing boat.

- Bonding with my spiritual brothers: Bubba, Big Chuck and Jimbo.

- Trying to avoid another fight with our neighbor over the real words to "Louie, Louie."

- Rehearsing a scene for our Community Playhouse production of "Moby Dick."

- Giving you some space and time to get to know yourself better.

Mary E. Hirsch

Rules For The Hunt, Minnesota-Style

It's hunting season in Minnesota. This is the time when you see grown men (and a few women) stand at the shores of our city lakes and weep at all the ducks and geese that they can't get their hands on.

My father and my brother used to go hunting with other fathers and sons. They would leave early in the morning in their wood-paneled station wagons, dressed in camouflage outfits that made them look like G.I. Joe wanna-be's. Outside of switching our Wonder bread for whole wheat bread, this was as primitive as a middle-class Minneapolis family could get in the 50's and 60's. I guess my mother and I and all the other womenfolk were supposed to stay home weaving fabric, churning butter, and making candles waiting for the menfolk to bring home dinner.

I don't think it's a coincidence that hunting season starts about the same time the elections begin to heat up. After all, a person can fill those endless hours spent sitting in a duck blind by reading political pamphlets and newspaper editorials. You might even lure an unsuspecting animal into your trap by promising it better housing and more DNR protection. Hunting is often a political controversy itself. It brings up issues such as animal rights, hunters' rights, land rights, the right to bear arms, and the right to tell stories about how a duck the size of an airplane got away.

A lot of people who have moved to the Twin Cities complain that life-long residents aren't friendly or helpful. So, as a public service and in the name of friendship, in case you are new to this area or are thinking of going hunting for the first time, take a little friendly advice – unless you want to find yourself in a world of trouble – don't say these things while standing in line to get your hunting license or sitting around a hunters' bar:

- "I think a good ballet troupe or an outstanding opera company could make all of us forget the Twins and the Vikings."

- "I can't even begin hunting in the morning without my cup of espresso."

- "You know, that orange hat really brings out the yellow flecks in your eyes."

- "I think the NRA is full of radical right-wingers, don't you?"

- "When you're out in the woods do you have trouble keeping your herbal tea warm?"

- "Have you read 'The Secret' yet?"

- "Want to sign my petition to make it illegal to drink beer while hunting?"

- "You know, leftover bear urine makes a nice aftershave lotion."

- "I just finished crocheting a gun cozy and I feel so fulfilled as a hunter."

- "This town doesn't need a new stadium, it needs more bagel shops."

- "Who would you rather hunt with – Ryan Seacrest or Richard Simmons?"

- "Would you like to hear some of the Haiku I wrote last year while sitting in a tree?"

- "I think my Toyota Prius is just as efficient for hunting as any old pick-up truck."

- "Keith Urban can't hold a candle to Kenny G."

- "The University of Minnesota should spend more money on research and development and less money on sports."

By the way, if hunting doesn't turn out to be your thing, don't worry: you soon can spend hours sitting in a wood shack, looking into a hole in the ice, and participate in the great Minnesota pastime – wondering if winter will ever end!

The Secret Language of "The" Cabin

The other day I was at lunch with some friends when I heard something I know I've heard hundreds of times before, but for some reason this time it finally sank in.

One friend said "I'm going to the cabin this weekend," followed by the comment from another friend, "I went to the cabin last week, but we aren't going back up until the 4th."

Now, being cabin-impaired, I'm used to listening to cabin talk (also known as "Cabinese") and every once in a while chiming in with a clever remark such as "I'm going to be putting Log Cabin syrup on my waffles this weekend." But this time it was different. I suddenly became suspicious that there are not thousands of lake homes up north like so many of us believe, there is only one cabin – THE CABIN – and the people who go there spend all their time mocking those of us who are stuck at home for the weekend.

Perhaps you are like the CIA, FBI and IRS and believe I'm slightly paranoid (have they told you that?), but haven't you heard someone say "I'm going to *the* cabin this weekend," or "I was at *the* cabin this week," and thought to yourself, "They talk about *the* cabin, but I've never seen *the* cabin."

And then when your friends think you may be catching on to the one-cabin theory, they use the most covert statement of all: "We had some friends come up to *the* cabin." This is a statement that is only meant to give credibility to the idea that there are many cabins up north and your friend has witnesses to prove it. It sounds like a cabin conspiracy of sorts to me.

And let's just humor the cabin people, go with reality, and agree that there are thousands of cabins out there; so why put an emphasis on "the"? Where is "our" cabin, or "my family's" cabin, or even "my boss's cabin" that he let me use so I won't tell his wife what I saw at the last Christmas party?

So I've decided to fight back and start using cabinese in my own life to make others jealous of my lifestyle. For instance, from now on I'm washing *the* clothes, bathing *the* dog, making *the* bed, staying with *the* nephew, running *the* errands, going to *the* movie, and shaving *the* legs.

I have a feeling when *the* cabin people hear about my exciting life, they will want to stay in *the* city.

The End.

Kindle The Fire, Rekindle A Romance.

Friends of mine recently decided to go on a second honeymoon. After 15 years of marriage, three children, two mortgages, and God-alone-knows how many tuna noodle hot-dishes (they are a good Lutheran couple), these two decided to get away from it all for a week. So where are they going? Not to Hilton Head or Honolulu or even Hackensack.

They are going camping.

Camping is a noble activity, and in my younger days (when dinosaurs still roamed the earth), I used to go camping every summer. Lots of people like to get away from the city and head outdoors for a weekend of camping, but it seems to me that pitching tents and pitching "woo" (as my Grandma called it) just don't naturally go together. After all, you rarely see a silk teddy featured in L.L. Bean or find bikini briefs at Hoigaards. When was the last time you saw a romance novel called "Sweet Savage Camper" or heard Tony Bennett sing "I Left My Heart In The Boundary Waters"?

But what do I know? In his recent best seller, "How To Make Love To A Camper," Dr. Woody Acres says it is possible to kindle a campfire and rekindle a relationship at the same time.

Here are some things Dr. Acres says are real "turn-ons" for today's campers:

- Mosquito netting underwear.

- Slow dancing to Captain and Tenille's "Muskrat Love."

- Watching a guy drive in a tent stake while crushing a beer can on his head.

- A chilled glass of Winnebago Wine sipped from a tin cup.

- Becoming caught-up in the scent of Bactine as your loved one cleans the laceration you got while gathering wood for the fire.

- Cuddling in a black satin sleeping bag for two.

- Watching the smoke from the dry ice rise out of a Coleman cooler as the sun sets behind the outhouse.

- Making love to the sound of raccoons digging through your garbage.

- The silhouette of a park ranger checking your State Park Permit by campfire light.

- The residue of a gooey toasted marshmallow sitting delicately on the corner of the mouth.

- A rousing game of Smokey the Bear and the Naughty Firemaker.

- A dab of mosquito repellent behind the ears, and in other strategic spots.

- A dove cooing as the warm summer breeze blows down your tent.

- The sound of teeth gnawing as dried beef jerky is savagely torn from its package.

It Can Never Get Too Cold

- Eating off the same graham cracker of a S'more.

- The never-ending slurping sound as a lover strives to obtain the last drop of punch from a juice box.

- Catching a whiff of Off as your significant other checks your hair for wood ticks.

Is anyone else getting warm or is it just me?

Chapter 7

Minnesota Hotdish
(aka A Bunch of Leftovers Thrown Together)

Yes, this is exactly what it says, writings that don't fit the other categories, so they get stirred up together in one great big chapter. Put a few chow mein noodles or bread crumbs on top and you have a literary hotdish -- and I use the term "literary" loosely and with full knowledge that many writers who take themselves way too seriously will be offended. Oh well.

Are You A Real Minnesotan?

Are you a real Minnesotan? In the tradition of Cosmo-politan, take the following test to find out just how deep your Minnesota roots go:

"I don't mind the heat, it's _____ I can't stand!"
- A. the humidity
- B. the Legislature
- C. the crowds at the Mall of America

"I don't mind the snow, it's _____ I can't stand"
- A. the freezing cold
- B. the Legislature
- C. being stuck in the house without cable TV

Minnesota's motto is:
- A. "L'Etoile du nord" or Star of the North
- B. "Make Lefse, Not Waves"
- C. "This road is under construction, be prepared to stop"

Politically, Minnesotans are considered:
- A. Liberal
- B. Conservative
- C. Plaid

A popular movie made in Minnesota is:
- A. "Grumpy Old Men"
- B. "The Mighty Ducks"
- C. "Malcontent Mallards"

The state grain is:
    A. Wild rice
    B. Wheat
    C. Beer

Minnesota is often called:
    A. The Land of Sky-Blue Waters
    B. The Star of the North
    C. The place where Prince lives

A popular Minnesota tourist attraction is:
    A. The Boundary Waters
    B. The Mall of America
    C. The Polka Museum and Bait Shop

Minnesota's state flower is:
    A. The Pink and White Lady-Slipper
    B. The Dandelion
    C. Pillsbury pre-sifted

The perfect hot dish topping is:
    A. French fried onion rings
    B. Chow mein noodles
    C. Aluminum foil

The state song is:
    A. "Hail! Minnesota"
    B. The love theme from "The Mighty Ducks"
    C. "The Beer Barrel Polka"

A visit to the state fair isn't complete without:
    A. Going to Machinery Hill, the dairy building and the 4-H exhibits
    B. Eating Tom Thumb donuts, Pronto Pups, and something on a stick
    C. Trying to avoid shaking a politician's hand

The state bird is:
    A. The loon
    B. The mosquito
    C. An extended middle finger out the car window

A night of high culture is:
    A. Attending a symphony at Orchestra Hall
    B. Attending a play at The Guthrie Theatre
    C. Going to a movie starring Anthony Hopkins

The state capital is:
    A. St. Paul
    B. Minneapolis
    C. 'M'

Give yourself one point for every question you answered A; one point for every question you answered B; and one point for every question you answered C. If you scored 15 points, you are a real Minnesotan. If you scored 14 points or less, you should consider moving to a bordering state.

The Minnesota Orchestra's annual Symphony Ball is not only a major fundraising event it is also one of the major high social events of the year. If you have to miss your bowling night or the only formal dress you have is the one you wore 10 years ago as a bridesmaid, then you probably won't be going to the ball.

10 Things You Won't Hear At The Symphony Ball

1. "I'm so happy to see we're wearing the same dress. I was wondering how it would look on someone four sizes smaller than me."

2. "I think the Wyndham Hill label should record more accordion music."

3. "I haven't shopped there since they stopped doubling the value of my coupons."

4. "Of course, I was hoping my daughter would go to law school and join my practice, but she seems really happy as a street mime."

5. "I could drive to work but I'd rather take the bus; it gives me a chance to meet new and interesting people."

6. "I could spend the winter in the Keys. but I would miss warming up my Mercedes and scraping the ice off the windows every morning."

7. "I sure hope that next Public Housing project ends up in my neighborhood. It will liven up the block parties."

8. "Yes, I serve Brie, but I think Cheeze Whiz really improves a buffet."

9. "I've found that once you've experienced a truck-and-tractor pull sitting by the mud pits, you're never really happy again in any other seats."

10. "Sure, Harvard's an excellent school, but I'm glad my son decided to attend the University of Madison; it's a real party town."

Headlines Your Community Newspaper Won't Print

Local news is always busy these days looking at what stories it chooses to report. Newspaper, television, radio and internet editors make decisions about which area news items to report or not report. While stories about ordinances, business trends, local residents of note, and politicians are reported with great frequency, there are stories that have gone untold.

This writer feels the Twin Cities community has a right to know what news they have been missing. So, in the spirit of commitment to provide news that viewers (especially Nielsen viewers) want to know, I am releasing the headlines of some of the stories that haven't been reported in local news venues. Then you, the reader, can decide if these stories should have been covered.

- Geese Mount Offensive Against Park Board Workers. "It's as if they know we are trying to reduce their numbers," remarked a wounded game warden.

- Local Musician Possessed by Spirit of Liberace. "I can't stop smiling and I have this irresistible urge to wear gaudy jewelry," claims the puzzled performer.

- Linden Hills Woman Abducted by Aliens at Local Coffee House. "One minute she was sitting there, celebrating the moments of her life, and the next minute she was gone."

- Elvis Spotted Selling Self-Portraits on Black Velvet at Uptown Art Fair.

- Amelia Earhart Seen Windsurfing on Lake Harriet. "Like wow, that dudette can really fly," reported local beach comber.

- 80-Year-Old Uptown Woman Gives Birth to Two-Headed Child of Paul Bunyon. "I don't know who's more surprised, me or Paul," said the stunned mother.

- Ghost of Lincoln Seen Shooting Hoops at Lynnhurst Park. "I heard him mumbling 'Four scores and seven points ago' as he shot from the three point line," reported a local hoopster.

- Jogger's Brain Stolen by Martians. Endorphin shortage on Mars believed to be motive.

- Swimmers Say Jimmy Hoffa at Bottom of Lake Harriet. "He didn't look good," observed one of the divers.

- Robert Fulton's Spirit Haunts Lake Harriet Paddleboat.

- Man Claims Lake Harriet Pump Water Cures Baldness. "Within a few minutes of splashing some of the nectar on my face and head, I went from Howie Mandel to George Clooney," revealed the pleasantly surprised follicle recipient.

- Local Scientist Discovers Lutefisk Improves Love Life.

- Windom Woman Unearths Remains of Prehistoric Chia Pets.

- Big Foot Spotted Rollerblading at Lake of the Isles. "If he hadn't been skating in the wrong direction, he probably would have gone unnoticed," said the park police officer on the scene.

- Kenny Neighborhood Psychic Claims: "I am Channel for the Spirit of Minnehaha"

- Lose 10 lbs. in One Day With Tangletown Diet.

- Spaceship Lands in Harriet Rose Garden. "They were in search of Klingons," claimed stunned witness.

- Abominable Snowman Invades Lake Harriet Icehouse. "I couldn't believe my eyes," said astonished angler.

- Government Documents Reveal Arctic Clippers Are Communist Plots. "As far as we can tell," the unnamed source said, "the Cold War is still blowing."

- Lynnhurst Home Haunted By Ghost of Leif Erikson. "I heard him wandering the halls one night, calling out Bud Grant's name," stated stunned neighbor.

- Local Dressmaker Declares "I Was J. Edgar Hoover's Designer."

- Elected Official Wants to Marry Mallard; Feathers Ruffled at City Hall.

- Armatage Woman Reveals "I Was Prince Charles' Love Slave."

- Mutant Mosquitos Carry Off Kingfield Kanine. "I turned my back for a minute and the next thing I saw was Duchess being whisked off into the sunset," reports the devastated owner.

Mary E. Hirsch

Minnesota Movies We Want To See
(Or Do We?)

The Minnesota Legislature is considering a bill that will provide millions of dollars to movie companies to film in Minnesota. Movies are good publicity for the state and good revenue too. Here are a few of the projects that are being considered for funding:

There won't be a dry eye in the stadium seating theater when ***Teamless in Minneapolis*** hits the screen. This story is of one man's struggle to deal with another post-season loss by his football team by spilling his guts on local sports radio shows.

Six men who want to buy a new fishing boat and are willing to do anything to come up with the money will shock the socks off their neighbors in ***The Full Monticello***.

Out of Iowa is a memoir of three sisters who come of age when their family moves to Minnesota and they learn that grass is for mowing, not for grazing.

How could it happen? Where were they going? When will they be released from the asphalt abyss? Only the devil could concoct ***Road Construction from Hell***.

Sent here to observe and learn from their earthling counterparts, these ***Mosquitoes From Mars*** truly become blood-thirsty when they get a taste of good old-fashioned cream of AB-positive hot dish.

In ***Return of the Red River Valley Girls***, six women escape from the Helene Curtis Detention Center and School of

139

Cosmetology and are headed for the city. Beware: these gals are packing perm rods, and they know how to use them.

Does evil lurk behind all that blond hair, blue eyes, and ski sweaters? Can people who gave us clog dancing really have nasty thoughts? Is there a mean streak in that stoic disposition? Yah sure, you betcha, **When Scandinavians Go Bad.**

The runny nose, the projectile sneeze, the watery eyes, the hacking cough. Only one person can help: **The Kleenex-orcist.** This two-ply thriller is snot for the faint-hearted.

The Anti-Freeze has come to earth and threatens the future of ice fishing. **No Country for Ole Men** is sure to scare the heck out of you.

What happened to the men who tried to enter the kitchen of Our Lady of Perpetual Windchill Church during its fall festival pot luck? No one will be seated during the hot dish scene of **Don't Go Near The Kitchen.**

We predict there's a chance of terror when militant meteorologists take over the local weather channel in **The Rain Or Shining.**

Radio talk-show host Clint Midwestwood gambles with his life in **Play Mystic Lake For Me.**

Get ready to pucker up and die when **The Chapped Lips from Hell** come looking for you. This sci-fi comedy is a good example of chap schtick.

It's going to be a long night for the game warden when

alien anglers come to earth seeking their **Outer Catch Limits**. The Department of Unnatural Resources is open for business.

She thought she was attending an ordinary poetry reading at The Loft. But she had stumbled into a new dimension of rhyme and space. She was in **The Recite Zone.**

They're woolly and they're flannel; Their basement has wood panel; They love to surf the channels; **The Plaiddams Family.**

Terror is on tap in **The Attack of the Beerwolf.** It's another full moon and another beer distributor has disappeared. This brewski-slewski is sure to cure what ales you.

Our woe's begun when **Keillors From Outer Space** invade Minnesota. Will they stop at nothing in their quest for above average kids? Will everyone be forced to wear red socks?

The neighborhoods around the MSP Airport have always had problems with the noise from the planes landing and taking off. I am included in the group of neighbors who live on the flight path. Sometimes the planes came in so low you can see the people on board. There was, and still is, a constant "conversation" going on between the airport commission and the neighbors who are still living with the noise.

10 Advantages To Living Near The Minneapolis-St. Paul Interenational Airport (There are advantages?)

1. You can get a part-time job with the airlines, notifying pilots whether their landing gear is engaged.

2. Your dog can bark all it wants and your neighbors never will hear it.

3. It's a good excuse when someone asks why you're moving to the suburbs.

4. Worrying about the financial woes of the airlines doesn't keep you awake at night.

5. You can make love without your kids (or your partner) hearing you.

6. You don't have to worry about hot-air balloonists peeking in your windows.

7. When visitors look up at how low an airplane is flying, you can take an extra piece of dessert without anyone knowing.

8. If you ever go deaf, you'll already know how to read lips.

9. You don't have to come to the door when some boring visitor stops by because you can always tell them later that you never heard the doorbell.

10. You can enjoy TV reruns because you never get to hear an entire show the first time it's on.

Honk If You Love Minnesota Winters

Bumper stickers are a popular form of communication. They are like graffiti with wheels. You can promote a cause, support a candidate, cheer for a team, make a statement or cover up a dent that you hope your spouse won't see.

I've been noticing the bumper stickers on cars in the neighborhood and have found everything from political statements ("Visualize World Peace" or "Protect The Right To Bear Arms"), to humorous satire ("Visualize Whirled Peas" or "Protect The Right To Arm Bears"), to statements about how many years someone has been a member of the triple-A or which team they support. There are a lot of stickers that tell me the person driving the car hearts this or hearts that. But these stickers are generic in so many ways. It would be nice to see some bumper stickers that had a little local flavor. For instance:

- Put It On A Stick And I'll Eat It

- I Brake For Lutefisk

- Leeches Suck

- Have You Hugged Your Hot Dish Today?

- Spare The Rod; Spoil The Opener

- Snow Survival Kit On Board

- Honk If You Love (In A Stoic Sort Of Way) Scandinavians

- It Will Be A Great Day When Our Schools Get All The Money They Need And Team Owners Have To Hold A Bake Sale To Build A New Stadium

- God Isn't Dead – Jesse Ventura Was Just A Big Mistake

- Question Authority – Unless It Wouldn't Be A Nice Thing To Do

- Don't Blame Me I Voted For Warmer Weather

- If You're Warm; I'm Single

- Will Yodel For Cough Drops

- I'd Rather Be Eating Lefse

- I May Be Slow But Soon As I Get My Tongue Off Of This Metal Railing I'll Catch Up To You

- God Is Coming – But Not Until Summer

- Pro Lefse

- You Mean The Ice Age Is Over?

- Save the Norwegians

- Polka Till You Puke

- Visualize Green Bean Hot Dish

- Minnesota: Where Frigidity Has Nothing To Do With Sex

- Practice Random Acts of Warmness

It Can Never Get Too Cold

- You Cannot Simultaneously Prevent and Prepare for Sven-harnas Dag

- Will Work For Bait

- Beam Me Up Scotty; It's Colder Than Heck Down Here

- Wind Chill Happens

- My Other Car Is Stuck In A Snowdrift

- It's 10:00 – Do You Know Where Your Space Heater Is?

- Honk If You Love Flannel

- Minnesotans Love To Get Down – Down Vests, Down Parkas, Down Pants, Down Comforters

If You've Got The Minnesota Joke, We've Got The Punchline

It always amazes me when people are incapable of laughing at themselves. In his book "*Man's Search For Meaning*," Viktor Frankl wrote "Humor [is] another of the soul's weapons in the fight for self-preservation. It is well known that humor, more than anything else in the human make-up, can afford an aloofness and an ability to rise above any situation...." When he wrote this he was referring to himself and the other prisoners at Auschwitz. As a humorist, comedian and swell gal, I can't get over how scared we have become of laughing, especially at ourselves. People were offended by the movie "Fargo" because it poked fun at the way people in Minnesota talk. I wasn't offended by a few "you betcha's," although I did find wood chipper scene a little less than rollicking.

Now I've said all that because I had planned on sharing a bunch of Minnesota jokes with you, but because I don't want to offend anyone, I'm just going to tell you the punch lines – you can make up your own joke. So here are the punch lines to some great jokes written just for you:

- I told you to pass your bait! Pass your bait!

- Gee – it tasted like Lutefisk!

- One to hold the ladder, one to screw in the bulb, and 25 to get approval from the city of Minneapolis.

- Yeah, well plow this!

- But officer, this is the odd side of the street.

It Can Never Get Too Cold

- The state Capitol, City Hall and O'Brien's Irish Pub.

- That is my action figure.

- Oh yeah, and the snowmobile you rode in on.

- Because the bride sat on the accordion.

- Sure you are, and I'm a golf pro at the Edina Country Club.

- Now that's what I call a hot dish!

- I didn't know they made that in plaid flannel!

- Now Lena, that's what I call a snow blower!

- Look, it's God's gift to Lutherans!

- Look there goes the artist formerly known as Bob.

- Johnson, Olson, it's all Scandinavian to me.

- Uff da yourself!

- Sure we'll get a new stadium, and I'll be elected King of Sweden.

- As cold as a clerk at the impound lot.

- Oh no, I thought it was Cream of Mushroom soup!

- M-I-N-N-E-I-E-I-Oh oh

- Is that a Ronco fish finder in your pocket or are you just happy to see me?

Minnesota Acts Of Random Kindness

Minnesotans are uniquely qualified to perform sponta-neous acts of kindness – those usually anonymous gestures that help make the world a better place for all of us:

- Give a bucket of bait to a stranger.

- Turn your teammates' bowling balls fingers-up when they aren't looking.

- Send a letter to a local news anchor thanking him for being Your Friend – then ask if he'll lend you a few dollars until payday.

- Buy someone a gift for no reason at all – then remind her of it every day for the rest of her life.

- Pick up the trash in your neighborhood – then find a neighborhood that has no trash and donate it to them.

- The next time you're at Ingebretsen's Nordic Market, buy a pound of lutefisk to be given anonymously to the next customer who comes in.

- Send someone as anonymous greeting card. Don't do it more than once, though. You may be treading on stalking laws.

- The next time you drive through a road-construction area, smile and wave at the MNDOT workers – using all of your fingers this time.

- Give a homemade craft project to a friend. Be sure to look for it every time you visit and express disappointment when you don't see it.

- Stand on the corner of 8th and Nicollet and toss your hat into the air until you've turned the world on with your smile.

- Hum the "Beer Barrel Polka" all day at work to give your co-workers a real lift.

Pickup Lines Of The Hunks Of Herman

The lonely farmers of Herman, Minnesota, became national newsmakers when they advertised for wives. After a year of searching, they learned the techniques of wooing women. Here are some of their pickup lines:

- Your eyes are the same color as my tractor in the moonlight.

- Have you ever dressed up as Betty Crocker?

- Wanna see my topsoil erode?

- Weren't you a model in the last "overalls" edition of *Combine Illustrated*?

- I hate these cattle auctions – they're just meat markets.

- I can't help looking at 'em – I'm a dairy farmer.

- I stopped watching TV after *Green Acres* was canceled.

- Sure I spread manure, but I have a softer side, too.

- I didn't mean to stare, but I was just trying to picture you in gingham check.

- Have you ever found yourself humming, "Thank God I'm a Country Boy" all day?

Romance Fiction, Minnesota Style:
A Frontal Assault On Love

Looking for some summer reading? Try curling up with a Minnesota romance novel. These stories are hot – without the humidity. Yes, try one of these Minnesota romances where love means you never have to say "you betcha":

- **"Norwegian In My Arms"**: When Lena unleashes her passion, it's "Ole, Oh Ole, Ohhhhhhhh le!"

- **"Skeeter Itch"**: Sometimes when love bites, you just got to scratch.

- **"Sweet Savage Bait"**: Alluring tales of the love affairs of Rebait McIntyre and the big one that got away.

- **"Rebel in Red-Plaid Flannel"**: Luke Lutsen was a charter member of the NRA (No Romance Allowed) until Helga Hansen came to town.

- **"Urban G-r-r-r-illa"**: Cal Swenson thought he had come to Minneapolis for a short visit, but when he met Mary Tyler Nelson, the problem became how ya gonna get Cal home to da Range after he's seen Mary.

- **"Wild Milfoil Nights"**: The tragedy of what happens when boats exchange water bodily fluids.

- **"Desire on the Docks"**: Women go for Billy Bobber's love lines like Walleyes go for leeches.

- **"Sultry Superior Seduction"**: When he's not working the boats, Milton is working the women.

- **"Hot Dish!!!!"**: When Ben Olson cuts the apron strings of Carol Carlson, nothin' says lovin' like passion by the oven.

- **"Torrid Cabin Fever"**: Snowbound for three weeks, Mel Miller's remote control batteries finally give out and he starts to see his Swedish housekeeper Ilsa in a new light.

- **"Sven in Love"**: Just when his rosemaling career is starting to take off, Sven falls for Lolita, the new postmistress in town. Is there trouble brewing? You betcha.

- **"HMOh-oh-oh"**: When Dr. Torkelson finds herself entangled in the arms (and sheets) of the hospital chaplain, she starts practicing mediSIN without a license.

- **"3M-m-m-m-m-m"**: When two executives start to practice nocturnal networking, Post-It notes aren't the only sticky things around the office.

- **"Carnal Polka"**: When socialite Tiffany Van Lamp hears the strains of the accordion, she trades her cha-cha-cha to oom-pah-pah. It's time to make whoopee, John.

New Cable Shows Could
Portray Life In Minnesota At Its Best

I've noticed lately that, with a few exceptions, the programs on our local cable stations have all the pizzazz of a cellulite commercial. After all, a person can only watch so many meetings of the county commissioners or city council without needing to seek professional help. It would be nice to see shows that not only reflect our community but are also entertaining. While this may seem difficult to accomplish, I have come up with a few ideas for local programming:

- **This Old Icehouse:** Your host, Bob Villa-Ice restores a discarded Frigidaire box into the envy of every angler on Lake Harriet.

- **T*R*A*S*H:** Each week we dig through the garbage of a local celebrity and try to find something we can call in to CJ at the Star Tribune.

- **Quite-A-Leap:** Here's a fast-paced game show where motorists try to get around and go over as many potholes as possible without needing to have their tires (and spine) realigned.

- **Bud Light:** You're in for a rollicking time when jokester Bud Grant trades his tacklers for ticklers and hosts an hour of stand-up comedy.

- **American Bandshell:** Come on down to the Lake Harriet Bandshell and be part of Sven Clark's weekly look at what's happening in the world of polka music.

- **The Jogging Gourmet:** Each week Chef Nike demonstrates how you can prepare a gourmet meal while jogging five miles on your treadmill.

- **I Love Lena:** Life is never dull for polka band leader Ole Ricardo, especially when he has a wacky wife like Lena.

- **Car Trek:** Come with us as we follow suburban residents venturing to the urban lake frontiers in search of Mother Nature, jogging paths, and parking spaces.

- **Call In The Family:** Every week witness the reenactment of an intervention by the family and friends of people who have become powerless over their need to fish.

- **Teenage Mutant Ninja Sunfish:** Four unsuspecting sunfish are transformed into fighting machines when they accidentally eat the Chia Worm they got for Christmas.

- **In The Humidity Of The Night:** The story of an underground subculture of people with hair that becomes so unmanageable in the heat they refuse to come out during the day.

Now these are the kinds of programs that may give you the incentive to learn to program your DVR.

Minnesota Superheroes

Look! Up in the sky! It's a loon! It's a Delta jet! No, it's Minnesota's Superheroes!

1. Faster than a speedboat with twin outboard motors, more powerful than the Ronco Fish Finder, able to catch 10 walleyes on a single line, it's **BAITMAN**, and he wants to have a reel good time.

2. Scandals! Falsified research! Lawsuits! Indictments! Nothing can stand in the way of **THE DEFENDERS OF THE UNIVERSITY!** They are B.A. mothers who will take no B.S.

3. She can bring home the bacon, fry it up in a pan, and sue you for discrimination if you pay her less than a man. She's **WON'T-BUCKLE-UNDER-WOMAN**, and you'd better cover your harass when she comes around.

4. Skeeters scatter! Flies flee! Gnats scat! Here comes **THE SWATTER**, and he wants to play a little squash.

5. *Cruising the state in their hotrod Zamboni, **THE WARROADIERS** will not rest until two-tier hockey tournaments are stopped and the color green is declared illegal. Get in their way, and the next penalty box you land in might be made of pine!

6. In northern Minnesota, you know that help is just around the corner when you hear, "Hi-Oh, Iron Ore! Away!" It means that **THE LONE IRON RANGER** is on the way, along with his faithful companion, **TACONITO**. If the bad guys know what's good for them, they'll mine their own business.

7. Wherever you find a pot-luck dinner without a green bean casserole, see a parade without a Shriner, or hear "Yes" instead of "Ya, you betcha," you can rest assured that **THE MASKED LUTHERAN** will be there like a bat out of swell to make all things right.

Scandinavian Wisdom Revisted

Much of Minnesotans' heritage comes from Scandinavian folks known for their work ethic, stoicism, and wisdom. These qualities are reflected in Scandinavian proverbs passed down over generations, but it might be time to update them a little. Here are our suggestions:

DANISH

He who knows how to beg may leave his purse at home... but if he goes with a purse, he'd better know how to fight or be a fast runner.

*The road to a friend's house is never long...*except during Minnesota's road construction season.

*Shared sorrow is half sorrow...*but shared underwear is a bad idea.

*The light and the serious go well together...*except at the Guthrie.

*A bad haircut is two people's shame...*but only one person has to walk around looking like a dork.

FINNISH

*The water is the same on both sides of the boat...*so why are the fish always biting on the other side?

*God did not create hurry...*six people sharing one bathroom in the morning created hurry.

*If a man knew where he would fall, he would spread straw there first...*and arrange to have a personal attorney with a video recorder standing by.

SWEDISH

*When it rains soup, the poor man has no spoon...*and his hair gets really sticky, too!

*No one becomes a good doctor before he fills a church-yard...*but don't use that motto for your clinic.

He who buys what he doesn't need steals from himself... but is a blessing to the Mall of America.

NORWEGIAN

If there were no fools, how would we recognize the wise... and who would buy all the lutefisk?

*That which is loved is always beautiful...*except first thing in the morning.

Top Minnesota Movie Downloads

Minnesota has been the site of some popular movies recently – *Grumpy Old Men, Mighty Ducks,* and *Iron Will* among them – that incorporate Minnesota and our traditions into their story lines. But many other Minnesota movies are "in the can" (or in the outhouse depending on your point of view) and they are popular in Minnesota. These movies include:

Midwest Side Story – When the Swenson's daughter Kirsten falls for Irwin Feinstein – Oyf-da, what a mess!

Dirty Fishing – Myron earns his living by teaching lonely, horny housewives how to cast off when their husbands aren't around. But when they start casting off their inhibitions as well, anything can happen.

Jurassic Park 'n' Ride – The story of commuters who mysteriously disappear after boarding an MTC bus that's been around since the Ice Age.

Lonesome Loon – A couple of aging truck drivers test their stamina when they lead their last convoy of Pigs Eye Beer trucks to International Falls.

Attack of the Killer Mosquitoes – Repellents don't stop them. Swatters don't scare them. Bred in swamps infected by nuclear waste, these mosquitoes will stop at nothing to get what they want.

Haunted Ice House – Killed in a freak auger accident, Charlie Parker has returned from the dead. But this time, he's fishing for filet of soul.

Attack of the 50-foot Doughboy – What started out as a bread-stick prank in the Pillsbury kitchens is now stalking the state for this Betty Crocker he's heard so much about.

I Was a Teenage Angler – Gus Gustafson appeared to be an average high school student, but when the full moon came out, Gus was transformed from Anglo to Angler. Only Babe Winkelman can help him now!

The Big Windchill – A dozen U of M alumni are stranded at a ski lodge during a blizzard and spend their days singing Motown hits with the karaoke machine.

How to Stuff a Wilder Bikini – College students on spring break head to Walnut Grove for a week of fun, fun, and more fun.

www.ingramcontent.com/pod-product-compliance
Lightning Source LLC
Chambersburg PA
CBHW071451070426
42452CB00039B/1050